Green
Faith

Praise for *GreenFaith*

"In this book, Fletcher Harper takes on the noble and critical task of inspiring and motivating the faith community to take action in caring for God's creation. He challenges stereotypes about the Bible and Christian theology in regard to its message about nature, and he explores many of the world's major faith traditions for significant practices and teachings on the environment. He shares meaningful stories from his work with GreenFaith that provide a window onto humankind's troubled relationship to the natural world. This book contributes to a growing body of work that shows the religious and spiritual element of the ecological crisis and the importance of the faith community's involvement in solving difficult environmental issues. Those who are seeking spiritual depth while wondering about the future of the planet—whether they are members of a faith community or not—will benefit immensely from taking the time to read this book and consider another narrative about the role of faith in ecological ethics."

—**Rev. Dr. Daniel R. Smith**, Lutheran Church of the Incarnation, Davis, CA

"From his very first sentence, 'Nature, the outdoors, the environment, is fundamental to religious faith and spirituality,' Harper makes it absolutely clear that religion and environment can be and should be closely linked. He provides a close reading of the Bible to demonstrate that environmental stewardship is, in fact, a central, though often overlooked, tenet of both Christianity and Judaism. Harper digs deeper, though, and explores the world's other great religious traditions and demonstrates that a deep environmental ethic is embedded in each of them. He explains that, 'To be a person of faith, a spiritual person, now means to love the earth as well as loving people.'

Harper's text goes well beyond an analysis of various faith traditions, however, and becomes a clarion call to action. 'We need to commit, and to act now. We need faiths to step forward, to use our collective influence in the service of this profoundly good, loving vision—eliminating dire poverty and restoring the earth.' In compelling prose, Harper explains the dire consequences our unbridled actions have had on the earth and all of its species, both plants and animals. He explores what is likely to happen if we don't act, and act soon. As he notes, 'The time has arrived for Christianity to recognize creation's basic dignity alongside humanity's.' But his is not a pessimistic message. He discusses numerous examples where religious communities have come together to make significant environmental differences and argues that together we can do much more. Together we can remake the world, if only we have the spiritual will to do so. Much of the impetus needed for actions of the sort most needed can be found within this provocative, insightful, and moving book."

—**Michael Zimmerman**, Founder and Executive Director, The Clergy Letter Project, and Vice President for Academic Affairs, The Evergreen State College, Olympia, WA

"Two generations after Aldo Leopold called for an 'ecological conscience' in his *A Sand County Almanac*, Fletcher Harper offers a context within which people of every major faith tradition, and no tradition in particular, can answer that call. He starts simply: 'No earth, no faith.' In the opening chapters he reveals how the earth is the gift that shapes our faith, and then in a pivotal interlude he gives a rich definition of *environment* that leads to the concluding chapters in which he presents realistic steps for shaping vision, encouraging economic development, and taking action. He makes complex concepts accessible and ends each chapter with provocative questions for every individual and group."

—**Rev. Phil Blackwell**, retired United Methodist minister, Chicago Temple

Green Faith

Mobilizing God's People to Save the Earth

Fletcher Harper
Foreword by Bill McKibben

 Abingdon Press™

Nashville

GREENFAITH:
MOBILIZING GOD'S PEOPLE TO SAVE THE EARTH
Copyright © 2015 by Abingdon Press

This book is printed on acid-free paper.

Library of Congress Cataloging-in-Publication Data has been requested.

ISBN: 978-1-4267-8175-9

Scripture quotations unless noted otherwise are from the Common English Bible. Copyright © 2011 by the Common English Bible. All rights reserved. Used by permission. www.CommonEnglishBible.com.

Scripture quotations marked KJV are from The Authorized (King James) Version. Rights in the Authorized Version in the United Kingdom are vested in the Crown. Reproduced by permission of the Crown's patentee, Cambridge University Press.

15 16 17 18 19 20 21 22 23 24—10 9 8 7 6 5 4 3 2 1
MANUFACTURED IN THE UNITED STATES OF AMERICA

To Lucy, Max, Mom, and Lisa

Contents

Contents

Part 3: Belief into Action

Foreword

We've had the Bible for several thousand years, and in most of that time the real action has been in the struggles of one human being with another. That drama has captivated us, in art and music and also in theology. Perhaps—we pray—it reached its crescendo with the awful, epic wars of the twentieth century.

But now a new conflict has come to the fore, the conflict between human beings and the world around them. It is an epic battle as well: this year we've learned that, along with melting most of the summer sea ice in the Arctic and acidifying the waters of the world's oceans, humans have also destabilized the massive ice sheets of the West Antarctic. That is to say, of the seven or eight great physical features on this planet, three are irrevocably changed. On land we watch the rapid spread of drought, flood, and wildfire, and we know that all are tied to our habits—that they're not, in the words of the insurance policies, an "act of God," but increasingly an act of man.

That's why it is powerful to turn back to our traditions and see—as this compelling book shows—that at their roots they have much to teach us about how to live in peace with the natural world. There are plenty of messages waiting to be discovered, in word and practice; they've been sitting there all along, but now that we need them we can find them and put them to use.

It's not as if these are secondary messages: the very first thing that God asks of those of us in the Judeo-Christian tradition is to exercise dominion over this earth, to dress and to keep it. Our dominion so far has been a pretty sorry affair: we're turning the generally benign order of the Holocene into overheated chaos. But if we pay attention we don't need to be a wrecking ball. Pay attention to science, yes, which puts definite limits on how much we can demand of the earth. But also pay attention to the delight we feel in nature, and to the sorrow we feel at its destruction. We were born to love creation; it's taken an act of will (thank you, Mr. Descartes) to divorce ourselves from it.

It's the great adventure of our time to try and reconnect with the world around us, and to do it with sufficient speed to save as much of the DNA around us as we can. It's too late to "stop" global warming or to avert extinctions, but not too late to minimize the damage. But it requires our species learning how to fit in to the larger whole, which is precisely the task we were assigned in Genesis 1. This slim volume is a handbook for starting that process—for the inquiry we need to undertake if we're going to be the people we've been called to be. If ever there was a book for its moment in time, this is it.

Bill McKibben

Bill McKibben is a noted environmentalist, author, and journalist.

Part 1
Earth and Faith

Chapter 1

Raw Awe

Religious Experience and the Great Outdoors

No Earth, No Faith

Nature, the outdoors, the environment, is fundamental to religious faith and spirituality. Human experience affirms this. The world's sacred texts confirm it. Human life and vitality depend on it. And, healthy religious faith is incomplete without it.

In regards to God, nature is as primary and fundamental as sacred texts. As primary and fundamental as our beliefs and rituals. As primary and fundamental as religion itself. Not more primary and fundamental—but as primary and fundamental for sure.

There's no spiritual life that does not involve, does not start, intimately and inescapably, with the Earth. That is not enriched and sustained by the Earth. That doesn't depend on the Earth for reawakening, rejuvenation, and renewal, for restoration and forgiveness, for life and love. Without contact with the natural world, our faith and spirituality are dangerously incomplete.

No Earth, no faith.

It's on purpose that this book starts not with the moral responsibility that spiritual and religious people have to protect the creation, but by exploring the role that the Earth can, does, and must play in our spiritual and religious lives. The Earth is a remarkable gift to our faith. It's in relation to the natural world that many of us have our most profound spiritual experiences. It's from the Earth that many of us draw a deep sense of awe and wonder, beauty and gratitude, community and love, and gain our first hints about the nature of God. The Earth is a gift that can shape our deepest beliefs in many ways, if we allow it. So it's right for a book on the relationship between Earth and faith to start by acknowledging this gift and by exploring it. By seeing what it offers us spiritually. How it moves us. What it teaches us.

Getting Past the Human Soul Alone with God

For centuries, a dominant image of spiritual life and practice has been the solitary individual, deep in prayer or meditation or in the study of sacred writings. Another widespread image is that of a congregation at worship in its sanctuary, a group of people gathered in its sacred place.

The suggestion of these images is that a spiritual life is something that takes place between people alone with their Higher Power, their God, their Source. Nature doesn't figure in either image except as a backdrop, an inert stage on which the most meaningful drama—between God and individuals—plays out.

These images no longer work.

They play into the dangerous and outdated tendency to view spirituality as something that takes place only between people, whether singly or in groups, and the divine. That it is somehow possible to connect with God outside of our actual being within the natural world. That we can, in some mysterious way, remove ourselves from the Earth when we seek oneness with our Creator.

On an obvious level, these images fail the most basic test of plausibility. We breathe, eat, and walk the Earth. Our lives take place in an incarnated context. And when we meditate or pray, worship and celebrate, seek spiritual aliveness and insight, we remain firmly within nature's embrace, even as we reach more deeply into the heart of life for energy and meaning.

But these images of the solitary human seeker and the congregation joined in worship fail for another reason. They fail because they treat the Earth, a primary source of divine revelation, as an irrelevant distraction instead of an indispensable companion. They're wrong because they ignore that the Earth is a gift that, very often, connects us to the sacred more powerfully than anything else. One of the primary reasons that people seek a spiritual life is because their lives feel pale, drained of vividness or energy or love or depth. Few things reconnect us with these energies more than nature.

It's time for a new iconic image of the spiritual seeker. A congregation joined in worship should be shown outdoors, appreciating Creator through and with creation. A sage, immersed in meditation or sacred study, should be shown in the midst of a field, embracing the divine in, through, and with the natural world. People should be shown in relationship to the creation. On a mountainside. At the sea or the side of a brook. Beneath the stars. Nature must be shown. Because it is always present. Because it very often represents the medium through which or in which people rediscover their absent vividness and personhood, the better angels of their nature. Nature is our spiritual companion and inspiration, the medium of our renewal and our vital energy. It belongs firmly within the definition of what it means to have a spiritual life, and to have faith.

Spiritual seeking without a place for nature is as inconceivable as spirituality without people.

Or without spirit.

Or without God.

Can You Recall a Spiritual Experience Outdoors?

In dozens of settings in churches, synagogues, mosques, temples, and more, I've sat with people in small groups and invited them, very simply, to recall a meaningful or spiritual experience they've had in nature. I invite people to sit. To recall. And to share.

It's a remarkable thing to watch.

My daughter Lucy, now eleven, used to play with those small compressed sponges which, when dropped into the water, expanded into an animal's shape. It was always surprisingly relaxing to watch those sponges grow. They remind me of human unwinding and creativity, exhaling and self-expression. They're fun.

Watching people recall and share their spiritual experiences in nature is like watching the same kind of process—in the flesh and in real time. It is watching the Spirit reenter human life. It's awesome.

Before describing the kinds of stories that I've heard most often, there are several things that are important to know about this process of reconnection and remembrance.

Universal

First, everyone has these experiences. I've spoken with groups of Jews and Christians, Muslims and Hindus, Unitarians and Buddhists. I've spoken with African Americans and Latinos, Asians and Caucasians, and Native People. Rich and poor. Young and old. Urbanites, suburbanites, and those who live as far from a city as they can. Regardless of their background or culture or social location or age, all of them have been able to remember this kind of experience. I've seen men in their eighties remember outdoor experiences from childhood that move them to tears seven decades after the fact. I've seen teenagers describe their first spiritual awakening taking place outdoors. Several years ago I interviewed people at an environmental conference about their spiritual or religious experiences in nature. After several hours of interviews with people from various religious and spiritual traditions, two men approached me. "We're atheists," they said. "Why aren't you asking us about our spiritual experiences outdoors? It's not like we don't have them."

To be human is to connect meaningfully, spiritually, with the natural world. Our capacity to experience the spirit in and through nature is a universal human endowment.

Close at Hand

Second, memories of these experiences are both easily accessible yet oddly forgotten. When asked, people usually remember these experiences quickly. These aren't repressed memories requiring great effort, decades of therapy to recover. In the small group exercises I mentioned above, I offer people one minute to recall their experiences. Most people recall them within ten seconds, and with clarity and vividness.

Yet, interestingly and sadly, few people have ever spoken of these experiences to others, let alone in a religious setting. For the most part, and for reasons we'll explore later, people feel it can be risky to share these stories for several cultural and theological reasons. But when people do try to remember, the memories rush forward with a sudden freshness. It's as if these stories are stuck in a closet in the middle of our conscious minds, straining to come out into the open. When the door is unlocked, they emerge bold and fresh, sharp and resonant. Even if they are years or decades old.

Spiritual Energy

Third, the impact of sharing these stories, and hearing others share them, is galvanizing and captivating. I've watched hundreds of people describe their outdoor experiences. When people tell these stories, they choose their words carefully. They inflect their voices as if their life depended on describing the inexpressible. They move their hands—jabbing at the air in excitement, caressing the open space in gratitude, lowering their tone in awe. It's incredible to watch, like watching the sap rise in a real human life. In telling these stories, people aren't just describing something that they've seen or observed. They're describing something that's become part of themselves, part of their own essence.

These experiences, at least in part, dissolve the human/nature divide like turpentine dissolves paint. What's left is a deeply integrated moment, a place in people's lives where they come together with themselves, the natural world, and the power behind it—all as one.

Variations and Themes

Over and over, people tell several distinct kinds of stories about their spiritual experiences outdoors. They tell stories about awe and wonder. They tell stories about beauty. They tell stories about relationships—with the human and the beyond-human community of life.

Awe

I grew up a Baptist and must have sung "How Great Thou Art"[1] a thousand times by the time I was twelve. I never really got it. Then, one summer, my Boy Scout troop organized a trip to climb Mt. Whitney. It was a very difficult, challenging climb. I had never had to work so hard physically as I did to get to the top of that mountain. But I did, and I looked around at the hundreds of smaller peaks that fanned out below where we were standing. I looked at a huge expanse of land. Then, for the first time, I could say "How Great Thou Art" and mean it. —Darrell

Awe: an emotion variously combining dread, veneration, and wonder that is inspired by authority or by the sacred or sublime. —The Merriam-Webster Dictionary

The first kind of outdoor spiritual experience people share is stories about awe, of wonder, in relation to the Earth. Darrell, who grew up in south central Los Angeles, shared a memory that exemplifies this theme. It describes an encounter with something that is physically impressive, that evokes a sense of the sacred. Many awe stories contain similar themes, though it's important to note that not all involve something of great physical size. The intricacy of nature's design, the intensity of outdoor silence or nighttime's thick darkness or a single, sublime feature of a tree can evoke awe. Awe isn't just about size. It is about a largeness of presence, whether physical or spiritual, or both.

Awe, in these cases, expresses our sense that we've encountered something far more full and complete than ourselves, a momentary majesty that evokes our hunger for a larger life. Awe captivates us and evokes our sense of our own limits. It reminds us that we're small, that the world doesn't revolve around us. In a culture that teaches that gratifying the ego is the pathway to happiness, it's notable that most people whom I've seen share memories of outdoor awe seem grateful to be reminded that there's something bigger than us. Perhaps we need reminders that it's a fascinating relief to lay the burden of our selves down.

Not Just Pretty

I was a good swimmer when I was in college, and I stayed in good shape into my twenties. I was swimming in the ocean during that time, and one day I thought I'd swim across a channel that looked pretty manageable. I got out into the middle of the channel, and the wind shifted and all of a sudden I realized I was getting swept out to sea. The waves were beating me up. I honestly thought there was a good chance I'd die. I remember feeling a huge fear and awe at the power of the ocean. Eventually I swam out of the current and made it back to the beach, exhausted. I'll never forget that. —Brian

There's another dimension to the awe-filled (or "awe-ful") outdoor experiences than simply being impressed and relieved. People sharing their memories often express, explicitly or implicitly, a degree of fear in relation to their memory of awe, tinged as above with a captivated fascination. While consistent with the dictionary definition listed above, this aspect of awe often gets lost in the pop-culture usage of awe that's focused on easygoing exchanges ("Have an awesome day!") or that responds to displays of computer-generated special effects ("That was awesome," my daughter said after seeing the movie *Transformers*.) As the swimmer above reminds us, *awe* means more than "cool." It involves dread.

The key to this aspect of awe is in the powerful, intimidating fullness of reality it represents. These experiences not only amaze us, literally. They seize us. They arrest our attention. They rebuke our sense of our own power. This aspect of awe reminds us of the relative vulnerability of our own existence. By reminding us about how incomplete, how small we are (again either physically or spiritually), awe has the power to overwhelm our sense of self—or at least to punch a hole in it. All of a sudden, the world doesn't revolve around us—it revolves around power that erupts through the natural world into us. "I have indeed spoken about things I didn't understand, wonders beyond my comprehension,"[2] says Job after God has rebuked Job's limited take on reality by revealing divine power through the panoply of nature.

There's an important message in this fearful aspect of awe. In recent decades, "fear of God" theologies have fallen out of favor, either because they've been used in manipulative ways ("God will punish you if you do this or that") or in a manner that repulsively defies belief ("God punishes gays with AIDS"). But experiences of awe in nature restore a deeper meaning to the concept of the fear of the sacred. There's valuable wisdom in knowing one's limits. Even in our Promethean age we remain mortal, and it's both terrible and a relief to remember it. Psalm 111:10 says, "Fear of the LORD is where wisdom begins; / sure knowledge is for all who keep God's laws," a suggestion that the regular experience of awe-based fear is good for us. Years ago, I watched a televised interview with one of the world's leading big wave surfers. The footage of him surfing down the face of massive waves was frightening to look at, let alone contemplate actually surfing. The interviewer asked him, essentially, if he wasn't crazy to do this. He responded that he thought many people had forgotten the importance of fear of death, of the preciousness of life. People took too much for granted, he said. He appreciated the fear he felt. It reminded him how grateful he was to be alive.

Nature-based experiences of awe remind us that there's a unique value in recognizing that we aren't the final word.

A Beginning of Religion, a Beginning of Ethics

A final aspect of awe requires attention. Many have recognized awe as one of the most basic religious emotions, a foundation for religious belief, an emotion from which reverence springs. Rudolf Otto, a renowned Lutheran philosopher whose book, *The Idea of the Holy,* a long-standing classic, established the idea of the Holy as "numinous," a characteristic he described with the Latin phrase *"mysterium tremendum et fascinans,"* ("fearful and fascinating mystery").[3] In Otto's view, the numinous, which contains the characteristics we've used here to describe awe, underlies all religion, and serves as its starting point, its genesis. Experiences of outdoor awe play this kind of formative religious role in many people's lives. These experiences serve as touchstones, entry points for God into our lives. Faith is born where these experiences happen.

But interestingly, awe doesn't only amaze us, doesn't just help us believe in God. It can also evoke our moral nature, our ethics. Think for a moment about a time when you've been in awe. One quality of such an experience is that it doesn't only astound. After the initial, adrenaline-driven sense of astonishment has passed, these awe experiences often make us more respectful, more reverent, more humble. Due to the depth of experience they provide, these experiences can help make us more honest, more compassionate, less destructive. Due to their raw honesty, these experiences help us strip away the falseness and shallowness of our own lives, and help us reach deeper than we normally do. Awe leaves a sacred pause in its wake, a time in which the soul is quieted, deepened. In that space, moral decency can be born. Theologians[4] have long recognized that awe is an important source of ethics, with many of them noting our experiences of awe specifically in relation to nature.

So, nature-based awe is not just the Earth's special effects provided for our entertainment. It's where majesty and beauty come together to evoke deep respect and faith, and to awaken our ethical lives.

Beauty

One summer when I was in my early twenties, I was doing a cross-country trip to the southwest. My friend and I were driving in New Mexico or Arizona and got lost on a side road. We just settled in and decided to sleep in the car or just outside. We parked and were sitting outside the car when the sun went down. It was spectacular with the colors. My friend went to read. There was a summer lightning storm on the horizon miles away. It was completely soundless, and the lightning illuminated the desert. I watched it literally for hours. —Luis

Beauty is a second common theme in stories of outdoor spiritual experiences. Like stories of awe, it is captivating to hear it expressed. The story above was told by a man in his late twenties. When he spoke about the experience, it was as if he was gazing on something so mysteriously rich that his words couldn't begin to capture it. And he was right. Actually, the beauty of the experience had captured him.

These experiences of beauty can, at a distance of years, remain remarkably fresh, continuing to serve as an entryway into deeper regions of the soul. In stories about awe, what matters most is the size and the power of the scene and, by extension, its source. In stories about beauty, what matters most is the attractiveness and artistry of the scene, not its size. The focus here is on skill and gorgeousness, not majesty and might. A different face of God.

When I go back home to Puerto Rico—that's when I feel it most. I can go sit on the beach for hours and watch. It's so beautiful. There are no words to express it. —Luis

Like experiences of awe, beauty evokes deep feelings with overlapping but distinct features. Awe-experiences evoke or even command respect. Beauty exerts a warmer, more sensual attraction. Through their unimaginably rich colors and strangely stunning proportions, their symmetric or haphazardly gorgeous design, nature's beauty is enamoring, enchanting. It enthralls with sumptuousness or sparseness or some combination of both. It causes us, in a way, to fall in love with the Earth. It makes us stare for hours.

Psychologist Erich Fromm, biologist E. O. Wilson, and others have used the term *biophilia,* (literally "love of life or living systems") to point toward this reality, our inalienable bond with our earthly home. Wilson in particular emphasizes the evolutionary value of such a bond for human survival, arguing that historically it's much easier for people to survive if they love the places they are—less stress, more happiness, more survival. There's much to like about this Earth-friendly theory. But by explaining this love in scientific and instrumental terms, *biophilia* has an unfortunate clinical ring (clang, actually). It tries to explain the depths of human experience with a scientific formulation. It's like trying to describe the meaning of a kiss between loving spouses by saying that it's evidence of a long-term relationship. It's not wrong. It simply fails to capture the meaning of a loving kiss that matters most.

The stunning film *Wings of Life* offers a flirtatious, more enticing reflection on how nature "uses" beauty to ensure survival. Cinematographer Louis Schwartzberg and narrator Meryl Streep team up in this remarkable story about flowers and the pollinators that ensure their survival—bees and insects, birds and bats. They describe—visually and verbally—the "seductive" power of flowers, which employ attractiveness of color, design, smell, and taste as their strategy for survival. Life, from this perspective, continues because of the depth and power of flowers' attraction. Because the flowers look, smell, and taste lovely. Because they are beautiful.

Another aspect of nature's beauty is that it has a unique style. The remarkable beauty of the flower. The perfect and unique bend in the arm of a favorite tree. The evolving color-tones of sunset or sunrise, or fall colors. Nature's beauty isn't like the beauty that's mimicked on a Hallmark card, a once-beautiful scene mass-produced, as if real beauty is something that can be Xeroxed. There is individuality to nature's beauty. It's always new, always surprising. Many sportsmen have told me stories about standing in their favorite stream or sitting in their duck blind, seeing the same space over and over, but different each time in subtle but beautiful ways. Ocean lovers know that no wave is exactly the same. Nature never wears exactly the same outfit. Instead—endlessly creative. Endlessly new.

Love

I live in Plainfield, New Jersey—a small city about twenty miles from Newark. It's surrounded by suburbs, but where I live it's a city. The homes are crowded and the streets are dirty. Lots of trash. I live about ten minutes from the church I serve and I walk to work every day. There's a tree that I pass every day, and it has one branch that's like an arm, bent up towards the sky. It's beautiful. Each season it's different but it's still so nice to look at, the way that it curves and bends. I hadn't thought much about spiritual experiences outside. But I sure do love that tree. —Juan

Often, the word *love* appears directly in stories of natural beauty. If ethics emerge in the wake of awe, then love emerges in the wake of beauty. Beauty has the ability to evoke love because it has the power to attract us, to evoke our deep emotional energy, to generate joy. Beauty draws forth from us the essence of the life force itself. "God is love," the Gospel of John tells us. Outdoor experiences of beauty teach us about an important dimension of that love, and its evocative power.

Love, here, is closely related to another religious concept—salvation. The reason? In addition to representing a great source of human fulfillment, love saves us. It saves us from meaninglessness, isolation, disintegration, and despair. Saves us from being alienated from life and from the Earth and from each other and ourselves. Love is a powerful bonding agent. Being bonded, connected, helps make us whole. There are few places where we feel more consistently reconnected, re-bonded to life than the outdoors.

Contact

> I live in a suburb of New York City, on a street with houses which each have a small front and backyard. Early one morning, I was getting my newspaper from my front lawn. When I looked across the street, I saw a large, red-tailed hawk eating a squirrel or a rat—I couldn't tell. It was mesmerizing. I looked at the hawk. It stared at me, as if both to acknowledge me and to warn me off. I felt like it was communicating with me. I felt I understood. —Lawrence

In small-group discussions where people share their stories of the sacred in nature, stories about awe and beauty almost always come first. They are powerful, remarkable stories, a joy to hear and to experience.

But there is a third kind of story. Almost always, it doesn't get shared until well into the conversation.

This third type of experience is like Lawrence's story above. It is an experience of cross-species contact, of feeling that we've connected on a personal level with the beyond human community of life. Of sensing that we've encountered another being, another presence that has a distinct being of its own.

These kinds of stories can be challenging to Jews and Christians, raised on the biblical teaching that humanity alone is made in the divine image (Gen 1:27). But whatever the meaning of that teaching today, it couldn't be clearer that people—many people—feel that they have had an encounter with the natural world during which they felt they were not alone. In hundreds of conversations I've heard these stories emerge over and over again. People experience a personal connection with an animal, a landscape, a place, a mountain, the ocean, a river, and it moves them deeply. Regardless of any past religious or cultural discouragement, people have these experiences. They will not go away.

> Once when I was a teenager, I visited the Cincinnati Zoo. One large gorilla was sitting fairly quietly in the back of a cage and I decided to watch her. I was taken aback when she caught my eye and held my gaze. I looked away then back. She was still looking at me and into my eyes. In a moment of realization, I felt consciousness within that gorilla, and at the same moment, read on her face a profound sadness and despair. I began to weep, and I felt understood the force of cages, prisons, slavery, confinement. She continued to gaze at me until I turned to walk away. —Kath

There's a simple reason that people don't share these stories readily. It's because telling them carries a risk. In our society, people readily express love for their pets and, to a lesser degree, for their gardens. Beyond these two instances, many people look down on those who speak about feeling personal closeness to nature, as if it represents an immature attachment or a form of emotional instability. It's not a compliment to be called a tree-hugger.

Consequently, people don't share these stories readily—who wants to risk sharing a story that will cause others to think poorly of them? And yet how sad it is that these stories, which have such humanizing strength, are culturally off-limits, the object of a taboo. If God, the realm of the Spirit, is trying to communicate with us through these experiences of cross-species communion, what does it say about us if we are unwilling to listen and to respond?

Not Just Animals

> Once I was in Muir Woods with someone I loved. Muir Woods is a national park of old-growth redwoods just outside San Francisco, and if you can't have a religious experience there, you can't have one anywhere. The utter wonder at the creature-likeness of those massive trees could not be outdone by human passion. The life-force of those woods, whatever it may be called—the woods just trembled with that force. Eventually we just sat, breathing, absorbing the spirit, the depth of life that was allowed. God was there. —Pamela

It's important to note that these experiences of expanded communion are not limited to contact with animals, or what we refer to as sentient life. People have spiritual, transpersonal experiences with trees, rivers, landscapes, oceans, deserts. These experiences happen all the time, with varying degrees of intensity.

For example, people feel love for places that they've lived for many years, a fondness of familiarity that is deeply personal. These feelings regularly extend to details such as the location of certain trees, the feel of customary winds and seasonal weather patterns, the smells of the ground, the ocean, plants, and more. Sometimes, people love their gardens or yards, the outdoor places where they have worked themselves. Others simply love places they see regularly. When I walk to my car in the morning in my condominium's parking lot, I look out at a marsh that's part of the New Jersey Meadowlands. I love watching the marsh, the birds wading in it, the seasons passing, the different patterns of weather and light.

When people leave these places, whether to move for work or retirement or for other reasons, they feel grief over the loss of relationship with their familiar natural setting. These feelings of sadness for the loss of contact with our home landscape are regular and real as is the comfort and love that people have, consciously or semiconsciously, for their home landscapes. But these feelings are not widely recognized, and their spiritual significance is not on the radar screen of most religious communities. It's as if, from a religious and spiritual perspective, these basic attachments don't matter, as if they lack relational and spiritual (and therefore moral) significance. Not only is this unfortunate from an environmental perspective, given that we tend to protect those things that we love. This omission renders us spiritually incomplete, as if we've stubbornly refused to value a portion of our souls.

People also develop a strong connection with places they've visited multiple times, whether for family gatherings, vacations, or other occasions. People frequently draw on their memory of these places to find a sense of peace in the midst of stress, to find healing and hope in the midst of sadness, or to awaken a sense of wonder and potential in the midst of everyday life, to be restored. "After my husband died, I kept thinking about our home in Hawaii," said one widow. "The water, the quiet, the air. It was the only thing that gave me peace." Some people even fall in love with certain landscapes or places that they visit, sometimes with an intensity that leads them to leave their homes and go live in that new location—an elopement of sorts in relation to the natural world. Whether through repeated visits or a one-time experience of a special place, people have outdoor places that are spiritually significant to them, that connect them with their more resilient selves. These individual experiences are, perhaps, part of the origin of religious pilgrimages in which hundreds of millions of people participate annually. Remembering these places is a form of prayer. It's like opening a doorway through which spiritual energy enters human life. But again, few religious communities pay attention to these experiences, despite their power to enliven and restore us in powerful ways.

Closer to the Earth, Closer to People

I grew up with eight siblings in a house a half block from a very large city park in upstate New York. As a family we spent as much time outside as possible, even if it was just sitting on our front porch on a summer evening. My family also had a summer home, "camp," as we called it, a small, five-bedroom, old rooming house about an hour car ride away, where we spent the entire summer. I loved it there! It was a whole new group of families and friends in a relaxed atmosphere where no one locked doors unless they were away, and we freely roamed through the woods in complete safety and delight. We climbed trees, raced salamanders, swam in a lake, and I liked to hang out at a stable and help tend the horses to maybe get a free ride. These were such happy times—not only being around nature, but around so many people that I loved. —Anne

If our outdoor experiences create bonds of affection between us and the Earth, they also often bring us closer to one another. In many of the stories I've heard, the natural world is a setting in which deeply meaningful exchanges between people take place. Family reunions, times with spouses and children, adventures with friends—all of these are enhanced, so often, when they involve the outdoors.

And though many people recognize the value and character of their outdoor places as an important part of their identity, we often forget how very deep the importance of these places runs. Several years ago, I returned to a place in Rhode Island where my family had gone when we were young. Though my father had died over twenty years ago, and though I had thoroughly grieved his death, I was amazed at the power with which my memories of him returned in those same places where we had been together decades before. The quiet beauty of these beaches and trails seemed the same, but emerged with the force of a long-ignored relative, eager to impress on me what I'd been missing. My emotions moved me to wonder. Was there some beyond-rational way in which these places where we'd fished and swam were a secret part of my bond with Dad, of the depth of loss that I still felt, of me? Not just a backdrop for the relationship, but an actual character in it, holding, protecting, and evoking memories from decades ago from an otherwise inaccessible realm?

Common Concerns

So far, the image of nature that's been offered has been largely positive, enthusiastic, and admiring. Some may find this overly romantic or unrealistic. Some religious people may be concerned that valuing nature highly is a kind of idolatry that, to quote Paul's letter to the Romans, risks worshipping creation rather than the Creator (1:25). Let's look at these concerns.

Romance or Reality?

Annie Dillard's famous book, *Pilgrim at Tinker Creek,* chronicles a year she spent in a cabin in the woods, observing the world and life around her. It's a beautifully written book. And it's a powerful depiction of the almost unbearable violence that exists throughout nature. In an early passage, she describes her cat returning from a night of hunting, paws covered with the blood of her victims. In a passage that juxtaposes nature's simultaneous beauty and savagery, Dillard describes how her cat's blood-covered paws left beautiful shapes on her bedspread, like little flowers. Elsewhere in the book, she describes an insect that gets its food, its sustenance, literally by eating the insides of other insects, while they are alive. Dillard finds amazing beauty and unimaginable destructiveness side by side in nature, inseparable. It's hard to be romantic about the natural world after reading her work.

A first criticism of this chapter could be that it represents a "selective reading" of the evidence that looks only at the alluring surface of nature and ignores its brutal, bloody reality. There's truth to this critique. For those who don't live off the land, those living in cities, those who are relatively wealthy, it's easy to fall under nature's spell, to see only the beauty and not the suffering or raw violence. And it's easy to forget. To forget that every time we eat, every time that anything eats, something else dies. Seen from this perspective, nature is violent by definition. Existence is inseparable from predation. Life doesn't happen without killing. Nature doesn't add a romantic dimension to life. Except for alpha predators, nature is a living nightmare.

For many people, this violence seems indecent and invalidates nature's ability to serve as a point of connection with God. Because of this inevitable violence, some argue that humanity alone, with our rational capacity and our ability to choose between right and wrong, is worthy of God's attention and care.

But this argument—that nature can't connect us to God because it is violent—is flawed for two reasons. First, the fact of nature's violence, just like the fact of human violence, doesn't mean that nature is condemned, but rather that it's imperfect. If we believe that God is a loving redeemer, then that imperfection doesn't stop God from speaking to us, reaching to us, being present in and through the natural world. We believe that people, in all their imperfection, can still serve as God's ambassadors, hands and feet. It's completely reasonable to believe the same about nature.

Furthermore, recognizing the death and destruction that's such a part of nature can reawaken us to the reality that we're part of a larger system in which life and death are inextricably interconnected. We cannot eat without something else dying. Our life depends on the giving up of life. There's no other way. Because of this, it's right for us to offer thanks before we eat, to acknowledge the life given up so that we can live. And if we stop to think about it, recognizing the sacrifice that allows us to live evokes a respect and decency, gratitude and perhaps a healthy twinge of guilt. One of the major threats posed by consumerism is that it eradicates the link between what we consume, the food, the clothing, and everything else, from its living source. Remembering the death that supports our life is a way of respecting that link.

The Christian celebration of the Eucharist reflects this reality directly. In this ritual, people give thanks for a life given up so that they might live, expressing their gratitude and committing to moral decency in the face of an overwhelmingly generous gift from God. This ritual is understood to express the same deep truth that we've focused on in this chapter—that there is beauty and awe in the self-giving power of God, a beauty that incorporates the violence that's part of reality into a larger story of redemption and life.

Impractical or Essential?

A second criticism of appreciating nature and valuing it more highly is that it's simply not practical, that people don't have time for this level of engagement with the natural world.

Without going into detail here, we'd suggest that the opposite is true—that without learning to respect nature, and without taking time, individually and collectively, to appreciate it, we're doomed to an unhealthy and perilous future.

As described above, the natural world is vital to the strength of our souls, to our spiritual lives. This alone is one reason that recalling these experiences, and building a strong bond with nature, is essential, not impractical. But there's also an environmental reason that building these bonds is so important. As we'll explore later in this book, the undeniable scientific trends show us clearly that the natural world is in trouble, that pollution in various forms will cause enormous, expensive, and harmful problems in the future if we don't change. Much of the change that's needed is change in business practices and laws. But for those changes to be sustained in the long term, we need a deepened culture of appreciation of nature. That kind of appreciation will come, in large part, from people recalling and remembering the kinds of experiences described above. Spending time appreciating these experiences, and reflecting on them, isn't impractical. It's absolutely vital for a healthy future.

Idol or Icon?

Prior to beginning my work with GreenFaith, I served for ten years as a parish priest. After I announced that I was leaving parish ministry to work for an environmental organization, I attended a clergy gathering. A longtime friend greeted me. After our initial exchange, he said, "So you're leaving parish ministry to work on the environment? You must be a pagan!" He spoke jokingly, and I laughed and didn't think much about this until I went to another clergy gathering ten days later. But when another friend approached me and made another comment that included the "p" word, a light went off.

Many Christians hold a beyond rational conviction that if people grow too close to the natural world, or express too much concern for nature, that they somehow cease being Christian and become pagan. This sounds weird—I know. But I've heard these "pagan" comments made enough in relation to my work that I know it's true.

This suspicion stands in sharp contrast to the attitudes toward nature that one finds in most Hindu communities, where nature is deeply respected and venerated, and viewed as a direct point of connection with the divine. Hinduism has a wonderful exuberance in its embrace of nature—more on this later. For our immediate purposes, it serves as a reminder that it is fully possible for the natural world to serve as an icon—a clear window onto the divine—without being understood to fully embody the divine.

Another religious concept that can help us understand our relationship to nature is that of the icon as it's understood in Eastern Orthodox Christianity. Since late in the sixth century, the use of special images in worship—icons—has been welcomed.

Despite several historic controversies, icons have been understood as a way to help people connect with God, as windows onto the divine. Orthodox Christians have distinguished between the worship and veneration of an icon, understanding the latter as a show of great reverence and respect. Surely such a spiritual attitude is an appropriate one in the relation of the majesty of the natural world.

A final example from Islam is relevant here. The Arabic word *ayah* refers to a sign or evidence that points to the reality of Allah. *Ayah* is normally used to refer to verses of the Qur'an, all of which are believed to point toward their source, Allah. But there's one other way that the term is used in relationship to nature as another sign that points to nature's creator. For example, the Qur'an reads "Among His signs is the creation of the heavens and the Earth and whatever creatures He has scattered in them."[5]

Clearly, it is possible to connect with God through nature without idolizing it. The world's great religions affirm it. Sir Francis Bacon, the sixteenth- and seventeenth-century philosopher, scientist, and early advocate of the scientific method, summarized this point well. "God has, in fact, written two books, not just one. Of course, we are all familiar with the first book he wrote, namely Scripture. But he has written a second book called creation."[6]

Spiritual Practice and Our Relationship with the Earth

The spiritual value of nature is, I hope, beyond question by now. So in addition to spending more time outdoors, what are some ways that people can reconnect with the awe, beauty, and depth of life that this chapter has described?

Here are two spiritual practices that I've found useful.

A Different Kind of Autobiography

Think back to your childhood. Can you remember the outdoor places that meant a lot to you? Places you played? Places you explored? Places you found feelings of peace or a sense of adventure?

Think of adolescence. Can you remember outdoor places from this stage of your life? Places where you tested your own physical and emotional strength? Places where you broke rules in order to search for or express your true self? Places where you yearned and loved as only teenagers can? Places where you couldn't contain yourself—and yet the outdoors helped contain you?

Think of adulthood. Can you remember places where a sense of awe overtook you and you remembered what it was like, really, to feel reverent? Places where you saw beauty, had no words for it, and simply gave yourself over to admiration or even adoration? Places where you found peace in the wake of loss?

If you're like most people, you can recall these meaningful outdoor experiences from each stage of your life, but you've never thought about them all at once. Never recalled them in sequence. Never realized their collective value, the ways in which they revealed the essence of yourself quite so clearly. Never recognized the spiritual wellspring that they represent.

One exercise that helps us connect with these experiences is the eco-spiritual auto-biography, an exercise used by a growing number of teachers and scholars. In this exercise, people recall spiritual experiences outdoors from different stages of their lives—childhood, adolescence, adulthood. They remember animals and landscapes with which they felt particular kinship. They recall an experience in which they encountered pollution. For an added level of meaning, people can also reflect on their own ethnic and socioeconomic background, and to consider how that has impacted their relationship with the outdoors.

In addition to the flood of memories this exercise evokes, we've also found that it gives people a sense of "nature's personality." Often for the first time, people who recall these experiences realize that the natural world has multiple meanings for them, different faces with different lessons to teach or gifts to give. People describe these roles in phrases such as teacher of respect, revealer of beauty, source of strength, giver of peace. Recalling these experiences connects people with a new kind of relationship with nature. For many, this exercise also offers a renewed relationship with God.

Slow Nature

A second exercise I've found useful is a simple one to carry out. In this exercise, people go outside, wherever they are. If the weather or the circumstances permit, they take off their shoes. Then, they walk.

Slowly.

Very small steps.

Breathe calmly.

Intentionally, cover very little ground.

Observe.

Take nature in.

Not nature's vast scope.

The details of the ground they're standing on.

Details of the grass. Soil. Rocks. Tree roots.

Breathe calmly.

One of the greatest threats to our spiritual lives today is the over-fast, over-busy pace of life. If you doubt this, the next time you're in a group of people, ask if anyone isn't too busy. I'd be willing to bet that no one raises their hand. This exercise addresses that directly. It provides a way for people to slow the pace of their perception, to observe quietly, to settle in. By moving our bodies much more slowly than normal, our souls start to slow down, and we become able truly to feel again.

Discussion Questions

1. In what ways is the Earth a gift to you? To your friends? To your family? To your faith community?

2. What is it about the Earth that is the most fragile in your opinion?

3. Do people in your faith community take environmental concerns seriously? Enough to actually do something about them? In what ways do you contribute to the Earth's care?

4. Do you feel responsible for your environmental impact? What do you believe God expects of us?

Chapter 2

Good, Good, and Very Good

The Hebrew Bible's Teachings on Nature

Ask most people to name a biblical passage on the environment and it's likely they'll draw a blank. Or, if they can think of a passage, they mention it with hesitation, because the passage is usually the following one. "God blessed them and said to [the human creatures], "Be fertile and multiply; fill the earth and master it. Take charge of the fish of the sea, the birds in the sky, and everything crawling on the ground" (Gen 1:28).

We'll return to the "dominion" passage later in this chapter. Suffice it to say that most people, certainly most environmentalists, think that this passage sanctions destructive human exploitation of the planet. They're wrong, but that's for later too.

Hidden Truths

The Bible is filled with teachings that affirm the value of nature, with stories that land solidly on the side of respect for the earth. Most clergy aren't familiar with these teachings. The teachings aren't widely taught in seminaries, and there's little accumulated history of sermons of these "green" interpretations of biblical texts, so there's scarce precedent for clergy to draw on. But that doesn't mean that there isn't a powerful biblical witness on nature's behalf. We'll explore that now, reviewing a number of Hebrew Bible themes and texts on the earth in this chapter, followed by themes and texts from the New Testament.

Made by God

> When God began to create the heavens and the earth—the earth was
> without shape or form, it was dark over the deep sea, and God's wind
> swept over the waters—God said, "Let there be light." And so light ap-
> peared. God saw how good the light was. God separated the light from
> the darkness. God named the light Day and the darkness Night. There
> was evening and there was morning: the first day.

—Genesis 1:1-5

The first eco-biblical theme, that God is the earth's maker, appears in the Bible's first chapter. Look closely, though, and you'll see that there are two subtopics within this overarching theme. The earth is not just created. It is created good. And, it is created with a purpose, for a reason. Let's explore this further.

Good

> God named the dry land Earth, and he named the gathered waters
> Seas. God saw how good it was.

—Genesis 1:10

Throughout Genesis 1, after finishing the daily hard work of creating, God declares five times, with the satisfaction of a skilled artisan, "Good," with "very good" thrown in at the end for good measure. The repetition is lyrical and unmistakable—you can't miss it. It can even seem needlessly repetitive. Remember this sentiment for a moment.

Many Jews and Christians are so familiar with this passage that it barely registers. And in our scientific age this passage, while beautiful and familiar, seems like a benign anachronism, a throwback to a premodern time when people looked with wonder on an earth they barely understood. But it's a mistake to discount or dismiss this repetitive assertion of the Earth's goodness for several reasons.

First, imagine life when this passage was first written. According to studies examined by the National Academy of Sciences, life expectancy probably did not exceed thirty-five years until the sixteenth century.[1] People were dangerously vulnerable to nature. Almost every person would have lost loved ones to natural forces that would have seemed far from "good," forces like drought and famine, infection, infestation, plague, and natural disaster. Think what this first chapter of Genesis, with its multiple "goods," might have sounded like to people of this time. It could easily have seemed irritating. Off-putting. Wrong. To any sane person, it was equally clear that the Earth sustained life and also took it away. How could the Bible, which has a track record of realism about human nature, give such a one-sided view?

There is one reason, and it is a cornerstone not only of Judaism, but of all the Abrahamic faiths. The Bible calls creation good because our ancestors recognized the profound value of the gift of life and of the world that sustained it. The first chapter of Genesis, by repeating it over and over, makes this clear in no uncertain terms. The ancient authors looked at the earth with awe, wonder, and fear, with hope and vulnerability and great dependence. They looked at the earth and they listened to God. And they heard a simple answer.

It is good.

The greatest theological liability most religions have in relation to the environment is that they emphasize God's otherworldliness or transcendence to a far greater degree than they emphasize God's presence within nature and the value God places on the created order. The Bible, right from the start, is unequivocally positive about the value of the earth. And, as we'll see now, it is equally clear that God not only thinks the earth is good; God also cares about our treatment of creation.

Repeat after Me

Think of the issue of repetition in Genesis 1 from the perspective of a parent. The things that parents repeat, firstly, are things that are important. Parents don't waste time repeating things that are incidental or secondary—there simply isn't time. Further, the things that parents repeat are not the things that their children accept or follow, but precisely the opposite. Parents repeat the things their children forget, ignore, or want to avoid. The things they disregard, whether to test limits or express rebelliousness. Repetition is a way to make sure that something important doesn't slip off the radar screen. It's a technique most parents use to communicate what they value, and to shape the conscience and behavior of their children.

Perhaps, then, the rationale for repeating the goodness of creation was to assert it firmly in the face of understandable ambivalence, to transform understandable skepticism due to the vicissitudes of nature into persistent gratitude. Perhaps, as this passage applies to us in our times, the repetition can serve to firm up our resolve to remember the earth's goodness in a time when it's awfully easy to forget that the food we eat comes from the ground, the water we drink comes from aquifers, rivers, and oceans, the air we breathe comes from the exhaling of plants. Perhaps we need this repetition of creation's goodness every bit as much as our forebears did, for different reasons.

Life Support

God said, "Let the waters swarm with living things, and let birds fly above the earth up in the dome of the sky." God created the great sea

23

animals and all the tiny living things that swarm in the waters, each according to its kind, and all the winged birds, each according to its kind. God saw how good it was. Then God blessed them: "Be fertile and multiply and fill the waters in the seas, and let the birds multiply on the earth."

—Genesis 1:20-22

If the Bible is clear that God made the earth good, it is equally clear that God made the earth for a reason.

To support life.

When Genesis describes the creation of the creatures that live in the sea, the author, twice, uses the verb *swarm*. In other words, the oceans teemed, overflowed, with life. Perhaps the biblical authors looked out and saw oceans so overflowing with life that they drew the only conclusion that they could—that God's purpose for the earth was to support life, a great deal of it. Over and over, after successive daily bursts of creative activity, the Bible makes it clear that God takes pleasure in the ever-growing diversity of natural systems, plants, animals, sea creatures, and more. The purpose of creation is to support these various life forms—an ever-growing number of them.

In the Christian New Testament, Jesus told his followers, "I came so that they could have life—indeed, so that they could live life to the fullest" (John 10:10). Most Christians spiritualize this saying, interpreting it as God's wish for our psycho-spiritual well-being. Genesis reminds us that there's a physical dimension to this abundance that God intends for creation.

Owned

The second theme, that the Earth is owned by God, also seems so theologically obvious that it hardly needs mentioning. But it's precisely because this theme of ownership is so religiously taken for granted that it's worth deeper examination.

The earth is the Lord's and everything in it, the world and its inhabitants too.

—Psalm 24:1

At first glance, this text appears benign, if not toothless. It's the kind of biblical passage that appears harmlessly on church calendars, superimposed on a staged photo of flowers blooming in a field, an ambitionless, calming use of the Bible. But ask an African American minister to name a biblical passage on the environment, and odds are this is the passage you'll get. Repeatedly, I've seen African American churches cite this passage as the biblical warrant for the protection of the earth, using this text far more frequently than their Caucasian Christian or Jewish peers. Look carefully, and I think you can understand why.

Read the words. Think about what they say and what they don't say, what is explicit and implicit. The simple assertion—that the earth belongs to God—implies that that the earth does not belong to people and, in particular, does not belong to a dominant race of people. And then think about the history of African Americans, brought from their homeland to alien soil against their will. Disallowed by law from owning land by a dominant race of people. From this perspective, the statement, "The earth is the Lord's" serves as a repudiation of slavery, a rejection of a hateful form of domination. This interpretation of this passage is far from toothless. It sounds an arresting, revolutionary note. By reminding people that, ultimately, the land does not belong to us, but to God, it offers hope to an oppressed people—to an underdog. And it does so with an edge.

Major Donors

Who am I,
and who are my people,
that we should be able to offer so willingly?
Since everything comes from you,
we have given you that which comes from your own hand.

—1 Chronicles 29:14

A second passage that offers an interesting perspective on the theme of God's ownership of the earth appears in the passage above. King David, the ruler of Israel, had fallen in love with Bathsheba while her husband, a loyal soldier named Uriah, is off at war. In an appalling abuse of power, David arranges for Uriah to be placed in harm's way and killed. Nathan, a prophet, confronts David after the fact and communicates God's judgment—that David will not be allowed to build the temple in Jerusalem, an accomplishment that would have represented the crown jewel of his legacy. That task will be left to David's son by Bathsheba—the soon-to-be king, Solomon.

David, like many fathers, was ambitious for his son's success. So, he proceeds to collect the natural resources that Solomon will need to build the temple. He conducts the biblical equivalent of a capital fund drive, calling on the people of Israel to contribute. And they do. Following David's lead, many wealthy Israelites give generous amounts of iron and bronze, silver and gold, jewels and more. The capital campaign is a tremendous success. Its goal reached, King David calls the campaign to an end. Such success would be the envy of most modern fund-raisers.

David then stands up in front of the donors to speak. Any good fund-raiser would tell David that this is the time to thank his major donors, to praise their generosity, so that they will be more likely to give on future occasions. Celebrate by telling people that they've done well. That they are good. That God is pleased.

Instead, David says, "Who am I, / and who are my people, / that we should be able to offer so willingly? / Since everything comes from you, / we have given you that which comes from your own hand." Many people are familiar with an older translation—"All things come of thee, and of thine own have we given thee" (KJV).

I can imagine several of the wealthiest donors listening to David, then turning to each other and asking, "What did he just say? Who did he thank?"

This passage is a reminder of the temptation we face to think of our possessions—in this case of the natural resources we control—as ultimately our own. And like the passage from Psalm 24, it reminds us that God's ownership ultimately transcends our own. Once again, the Bible takes the concept of divine ownership of creation and affirms it, with an edge.

Our Property, God's Property

To reconcile this theme of divine ownership with the realities of modern life, it's important to explore the interaction between God's ultimate ownership of the earth and our use and control of the same. It's not enough simply to say, "God owns it" and to expect that to solve anything. Let's dig deeper.

Across the span of time, people have developed family, cultural, and social institutions, government structures, laws, and regulations through which they control and manage natural resources. Tribal peoples often relied on family or clan-based systems. In the middle ages, kings, rulers, and many religious groups controlled large natural resource holdings. In the former Communist bloc, governments were the major owners of "natural capital." Today, corporations control much of the Earth's productive capacity, alongside governments and individual landowners. Throughout our history, human beings have developed these different systems of ownership, use, and control over nature. In the face of this, what does it mean to assert God's ultimate ownership of the earth?

I'd suggest that God's ultimate ownership, in the face of our proximate ownership and control, matters deeply as a statement of our responsibility, our accountability, on both individual and systemic levels. Certainly God understands that as human societies evolve, our systems for the use of nature will evolve correspondingly. The issue, regardless of the system, is the underlying question of our stewardship. Is our systemic use of water and the atmosphere, our treatment of the land and of other living beings, consistent with what God expects? Do our systems of ownership and control of natural resources reflect the divine imperative that we respect and love creation and affirm its goodness by ensuring that it supports abundant life? It's not only our individual behavior that matters in relation to the environment. The systems that we develop matter too. If we believe that God is the Creator and owner of the earth, then that means we're accountable to God, individually and collectively, for the way in which we treat the earth.

When it comes to our treatment of the environment, we matter and our systems matter. There's no way around it.

Hitched

From all living things—from all creatures—you are to bring a pair, male and female, into the ark with you to keep them alive. From each kind of bird, from each kind of livestock, and from each kind of everything that crawls on the ground—a pair from each will go in with you to stay alive.

—Genesis 6:19-20

God said to Noah and to his sons with him, "I am now setting up my covenant with you, with your descendants, and with every living being with you—with the birds, with the large animals, and with all the animals of the earth, leaving the ark with you. I will set up my covenant with you so that never again will all life be cut off by floodwaters. There will never again be a flood to destroy the earth."

—Genesis 9:8-11

Over the past forty years, fundamentalist religions have grown rapidly around the world. Almost every religion has its own fundamentalist wing, but one belief that most of them share is a belief that a violent confrontation between good and evil is at hand, and that the earth will suffer enormous destruction as this battle plays out. The implication of this belief is that God views the Earth as a disposable stage or prop for the human-on-human main event. It's almost like the Earth is a ring for a World Wrestling Federation SmackDown.

The Bible teaches that God has a different intention for the fate of the Earth. In the story of Noah's ark, God is preparing to pass judgment on a human race that's gone badly off the rails by cleansing the planet with a titanic flood. But God makes it clear that, as well as saving the few decent people left on the planet, that the rest of the community of living beings will also be saved. Two by two, God has every kind of creature march into the ark, saved for a God-blessed future.

And at the end of the story of Noah, God makes a covenant, an unbreakable commitment never again to destroy the earth by a flood. But the covenant isn't just with people. It's with every living creature.

When it comes to the earth, God is hitched, committed, and not just to us. God is committed to the full community of life.

Once, while giving a children's sermon on this story, I asked the children why God saved the animals. "Because they didn't do anything wrong," one boy ventured. That works for me.

Biblical Biodiversity

If you come across a bird's nest along your way, whether in a tree or on the ground, with baby birds or eggs, and the mother is sitting on the baby birds or eggs, do not remove the mother from her young. You must let the mother go, though you may take the young for yourself so that things go well for you and so you can prolong your life.

—Deuteronomy 22:6-7

If the story of Noah isn't enough to convince you that God cares deeply about the diversity of life, the Torah contains this interesting passage. Rabbi Lawrence Troster, a leading Jewish eco-theologian, notes that "Our ancestors could not have anticipated the loss of biodiversity that the modern world has produced; from their perspective, there was no natural extinction rate of species. God, they believed, had created all species at one time and there could be no new creatures. Only humans could cause extinction." He then quotes Nachmanides, a thirteenth-century Jewish theologian, who commented on the Deuteronomy passage quoted above and a similar passage from the biblical book of Leviticus.

> This also is an explanatory commandment of the prohibition you shall not kill it [the mother] and its young both in one day (Lev 22:28). The reason for both [commandments] is that we should not have a cruel heart and not be compassionate, or it may be that Scripture does not permit us to destroy a species altogether, although it permits slaughter [for food] within that group. Now the person who kills the mother and the young in one day..., [it is regarded] as though they have destroyed that species.[2]

The biblical authors understood full well how easy it was for people to view the natural world solely through utilitarian eyes and to treat it only as a means of satisfying human desires. Their repeated insistence on nature's goodness, its right to exist for its own sake and for God's sake, is even more compelling when we consider the degree to they were so much more vulnerable to nature than we are today.

Awesome

When I look up at your skies,
at what your fingers made—
the moon and the stars
that you set firmly in place—
what are human beings
that you think about them;
what are human beings
that you pay attention to them?

—Psalm 8:3-4

The natural world serves as a primary source of awe for many people, and that awe serves as a gateway to a spiritual life. This passage, from Psalm 8, represents a biblical expression of that sentiment. The psalm's author is looking up at the vault of the heavens and sees the star-studded sky and the Milky Way, a sight that more and more of us can't access because of light pollution.

The author's response? The biblical equivalent of "Wow."

There's another biblical passage that evokes awe at creation and Creator. It's a long one, but it's worth it.

Where were you when I laid the earth's foundations?
Tell me if you know.
Who set its measurements? Surely you know.
Who stretched a measuring tape on it?
On what were its footings sunk;
who laid its cornerstone,
while the morning stars sang in unison
and all the divine beings shouted?
Who enclosed the Sea behind doors
when it burst forth from the womb,
when I made the clouds its garment,
the dense clouds its wrap....
In your lifetime have you commanded the morning,
informed the dawn of its place
so it would take hold of earth by its edges

29

and shake the wicked out of it?...
Have you surveyed earth's expanses?
Tell me if you know everything about it....
Can you hunt prey for the lion
or fill the cravings of lion cubs?...
Who provides food for the raven
when its young cry to God,
move about without food?
Do you know when mountain goats give birth;
do you observe the birthing of does?...
Who freed the wild donkey,
loosed the ropes of the onager
to whom I gave the desert as home,
his dwelling place in the salt flats?...
Did you give strength to the horse,
clothe his neck with a mane?

—Job 38:4-9, 12-13, 18, 39, 41; 39:1, 5-6, 19

The book of Job tells the story of a good man who suffers horribly and who tries to make sense of it. The book frames the story as God's testing of Job. It's an easy story to identify with, because so many of us feel that we struggle more than we should have to. As Buddhism teaches, life is suffering. Job is a story that validates this basic reality.

Much of the book of Job is taken up with Job's desperate friends trying to convince him that life doesn't involve suffering, or that if it does, it's Job's own fault. None of this works—it rarely does for us, and there's no reason Job should be an exception. Job is remarkably patient, with his own friends and with God. But, like most of us, he reaches a breaking point. He's had enough, and he calls God out, accusing God of ruining his life. His suffering is grave enough—loss of health, of wealth, of family—that it's easy to be sympathetic to his complaint.

God's response, the longest uninterrupted speech of the deity in the entire Bible, is unsympathetic and, literally, wild. God responds to Job not with solicitous pity, but with a bold, powerful, moving assertion of the deep mystery that lies behind our existence. But see how God asserts this. It's not with philosophical abstractions like, "I am God who dwells in eternity, who is perfection, and who is beyond comprehension," or some other mystifying response like that. Rather, it's by describing the natural world in great detail, its complexity, its beauty, its intricacy, its majesty. With this virtuosic series of verbal images that invoke different parts of the creation, God essentially reorients Job from self-centered to creation-aware. That awareness, that reconnection with the awe that comes from a genuine reckoning with the earth, saves Job from his own justified, but ultimately unhelpful, self-pity. Read the excerpts of God's speech above—or go to the Bible and read the full version, which goes on much longer. By describing creation with a fresh, dizzyingly multiperspectival vividness, God connects Job with the reality that there is much more to life, more beauty, more complexity, more gloriousness, more strangeness, than we can appreciate. In Job's case, awe at creation leads to renewed gratitude for life.

Several great theologians have described sin as our being "curved in on ourselves." This passage from Job reminds us that the earth is one of the best remedies for our own "inward-looking eyeballs."

Knowing Our Place

Rabbinic scholars have long viewed the passages from Psalm 8, Job, and others as having the intended effect of reminding us of our place in the larger order of the universe, evoking an authentic humility. Rabbi Troster has written that being struck by such nature-evoked humility and awe "can be understood as the fulfillment of the commandments to love and to fear God."[3] He continues by quoting Rabbi Moses Maimonides, the eleventh and twelfth-century Jewish scholar who remains one of the most influential of all time on this topic.

> When a person observes God's works and God's great and marvelous creatures, and they see from them God's wisdom that is without estimate or end, immediately they will love God, praise God and long with a great desire to know God's Great Name....And when a person thinks about these things they draw back and are afraid and realizes that they are small, lowly and obscure, endowed with slight and slender intelligence, standing in the presence of God who is perfect in knowledge.[4]

In recent decades, theologies that emphasize the fear of God have fallen from favor in many quarters. Experiences of nature-based awe, which often contain some element of fear, and the biblical passages that record these experiences, serve as reminders that the fear of God can still serve as the beginning of wisdom.[5]

How Does a Mountain Pray?

Praise the Lord from the earth,
you sea monsters and all you ocean depths!
Do the same, fire and hail, snow and smoke,
stormy wind that does what God says!
Do the same, you mountains, every single hill,
fruit trees, and every single cedar!

Do the same, you animals—wild or tame—
you creatures that creep along and you birds that fly!

—Psalm 148:7-10

Years ago, I was fishing in the northern Rocky Mountains at sunset. Standing in the river as the sun went down, I looked up at a distant, massive ridgeline. The fading sun was reflecting off the face of the mountains, and they were turning a light magenta. For the first time, I understood the line from "America the Beautiful"— "purple mountain majesties."

But there was more. It wasn't just beautiful and it wasn't just awesome, though it was both. I had a weird yet natural sense that the mountain was, silently, offering praise. Praise to beauty. Praise in awe. Praise in adoration.

It's very easy to discount this as an irrational, romantic flight of imagination. It's easy to say that my thought was a vestige of an obsolete, superstitious, prescientific time in which people thought that everything was alive. And this would be as useful a response as saying that falling in love is wrong or misguided because it's irrational.

There is a vital, mysterious interconnectedness to creation. There are times when we feel deeply, vitally part of something much bigger than ourselves, something indescribably alive. Psalm 148 speaks to this mysterious sense of community, continuity, and communion. Look at the verses above. Everything is joined in a collective praise of its Creator, its source. Plants and animals. Oceans and mountains. Weather patterns, atmosphere, and the wind, with its untamed freedom. The psalm affirms that we all share a common source, a common origin, a common starting and ending point. That's part of the meaning of the word *God*.

We know, in our heads, that we are all connected—all people, all the earth. That we have a common source and a common fate. Psalm 148 makes that knowledge emotionally real, celebrating this sense of community and of shared origin in words of arresting praise.

Who's Got the Power?

Now, it's time to circle back toward the "dominion" passage in Genesis, the passage mentioned earlier that gives so many environmentalists fits because they think it sanctions exploitation of the earth. This passage, like the important one we'll look at first, gives a job description for people in relation to the planet. Let's see what the Bible says in this regard.

The LORD God took the human and settled him in the garden of Eden
to farm it and to take care of it.

—Genesis 2:15

Farm and take care of. These words, which are at the heart of the Bible's second creation story in Genesis 2, offer a succinct synopsis of what we're meant to do in relation to creation.

Farm

Evangelical environmentalist Cal DeWitt has examined the Hebrew words that lie behind these English translations. Farm (which was often translated as "till" in older English versions of the Bible) is a verb that is used biblically in both agricultural and nonagricultural contexts. When it's used nonagriculturally, it is translated from Hebrew into English as *serve,* a meaning that provides an important clue to understanding the connotation of the word's deeper meaning. Jews and Christians alike are familiar with a famous use of this verb translated like this, when in Joshua 24:15, Joshua famously says, "But my family and I will serve the LORD." Or, in the more familiar translation, "As for me and my house, we will serve the LORD" (KJV).

Taking Care

This word (transliterated "shamar") has numerous rich Hebrew meanings, including *guard, protect,* and *watch over.* One of the best-known blessings in the Bible, which God has Moses teach to his brother Aaron, the overseer of the priests of Israel, goes like this:

The LORD bless you and protect you.
The LORD make his face shine on you and be gracious to you.
The LORD lift up his face to you and grant you peace.

—Numbers 6:24-26

It's a beautiful blessing, resonant with love and protective care. And one of its key verbs that expresses God's care for us, the verb translated *protect,* is the same verb used in Genesis 2:15 to express the care we owe to the earth.

Farm and take care of. Serve and protect. Knowing the connotations of these verbs makes the connotations of our job description crystal clear. We're not here simply to treat the earth as an inert, lifeless, inexhaustible store of resources to use as we please. We're not meant to be factory farmers. We're to offer protective service, to work with the Earth in the same kind of caring way that God works with us in our lives. Genesis 2:15 isn't a job description that sanctions our becoming a recipe for environmental disaster. No—it actually uses language that combines the protective love that we offer to our family and the skillful care with which we approach work we truly care about—our vocation, our chosen craft. "Farm and take care of" is a job description that calls for our excellence—our excellence in caring, and our excellence in skillful work. For God's Earth, nothing else will do.

What Kind of Dominion?

> *God created humanity in God's own image,*
> *in the divine image God created them,*
> *male and female God created them.*
> *God blessed them and said to them, "Be fertile and multiply; fill the*
> *earth and master it. Take charge of the fish of the sea, the birds in the*
> *sky, and everything crawling on the ground."*

> —Genesis 1:27-28

Fortified with the energy and commitment to excellence generated by "farm and take care of," it's now time to ask what "take charge," traditionally translated as "dominion" (KJV), really means. The first order of business is to dismiss any idea that the power and control that "take charge" implies can be explained away by exploring the original Hebrew. The Hebrew verb (transliterated *radah*) is a power word. It means what it says in English. It implies strength, raw strength. Nothing more and nothing less.

As I've noted before, this makes many environmentalists nervous. It makes them nervous because they think that this passage sanctions, blesses, or encourages us to exploit the planet in any way we want. Some have suggested that this passage is the smoking gun for the environmental crises we face, that it represents a baldly abusive assertion about our relationship to nature. Take no prisoners. Do what you want. Nature is here for your use—and abuse.

But reading the passage this way is a mistake. To be certain, the passage asserts that we have power. But it doesn't order us to misuse that power—it simply says that we have it. And that's hard to argue with. It's pretty clear that there's no species on the planet that has anything like the power that we've got. Humanity is altering every major ecosystem on the planet—the atmosphere, the oceans, and everything in between. Given our increasing numbers and our ever-larger footprint on the planet, this will continue to be the case. The genie is out of the bottle. We've got the power. To deny this is ludicrous.

But it isn't ludicrous to suggest that this passage confronts us with a challenging question hidden within this affirmation of our strength. The challenge is this: how will we use our power? Will we use it constructively and caringly? Or will our influence be characterized by selfish, shortsighted greed? That's the question we have to answer, and God can't answer it for us.

34

That's the real power of this passage. That's its real gift. Genesis doesn't sanction our misuse of nature. It says that we've got power, and that God wants us to live in loving harmony with the planet, using its resources with skill, responsibility, and care. It's for us to navigate between that first assertion of power in Genesis 1 and the vision of responsible care in Genesis 2:15.

Power, like money or any other source of earthly strength, is morally neutral. It can be used for good or for ill. When it comes to the environment, we have to choose, fully aware that we are accountable to God for the results of our decision.

Waste Not!

Now if you have been attacking a city for some time, fighting against it and trying to conquer it, don't destroy its trees by cutting them down with axes. You can eat from those trees; don't cut them down! Do you think a tree of the field is some sort of warrior to be attacked by you in battle?

—Deuteronomy 20:19

Another biblical passage, familiar to Jewish environmentalists and completely foreign to most Christians, serves to emphasize further the idea that, in God's opinion, there are clear limits on humanity's use of nature. The above passage, a centerpiece of Jewish environmental ethics, appears right in the middle of the laws in the Torah that govern conduct during wartime, the biblical equivalent of military "rules of engagement." Not exactly the place you'd expect to find a foundational environmental teaching.

In its original form, the law, quoted above, prohibits Israelite armies from cutting down fruit trees when they are laying siege to a city in wartime. But the rabbis of the period between 200–500 BCE expanded the application of this law, introducing an interpretive arc that has continued till today. They argued that this passage shouldn't only be understood in its original narrow context but rather as a prohibition against needless destruction or waste.

This interpretation of this law—referred to as *bal taschit,* Hebrew for "do not destroy," has found support from rabbis across the centuries. One traditional text asserts that wasting fuel or oil represented a violation of this commandment.[6] A thirteenth- and fourteenth-century rabbi from Spain argued that wasting water violated this commandment; many others declare that wasting food is a Torah violation. The influential nineteenth-century German Rabbi Samson Raphael Hirsch argued passionately that this commandment represented the most serious of warnings to humans "not to misuse the position which G-d has given them as masters of the world and its matter through capricious, passionate, or merely thoughtless wasteful destruction of anything on earth."[7] He continued,

> If...you should regard the beings beneath you as objects without rights, not per-
> ceiving G-d who created them,...then G-d's call proclaims to you, "Do not destroy
> anything!"...However, if you destroy, if you ruin, at that moment you are not a
> human...and have no right to the things around you. I lent them to you for wise
> use only; never forget that I lent them to you....In truth, there is no one nearer
> to idolatry than one who can disregard the fact that all things are the creatures
> and property of G-d, and who then presumes to have the right, because he has the
> might, to destroy them according to a presumptuous act of will. Yes, that one is
> already serving the most powerful idols—anger, pride, and above all ego, which in
> its passion regards itself as the master of things.[8]

Not wasting represents a powerful capstone theme for our treatment of the environment. It's moving to read the passion of the rabbis, writing in premodern times before the environmental crisis existed, or could even be imagined. Think of how they would thunder at us if they were alive today.

More to Come
Yes, the sparrow too has found a home there;
the swallow has found herself a nest
where she can lay her young beside your altars,
LORD of heavenly forces, my king, my God!

—Psalm 84:3

We've explored several introductory biblical themes and passages in this chapter, themes related to creation's goodness and purpose, God's ownership of the Earth, and the challenge this poses to our systems of control, our awe at nature, our role in treating the Earth caringly and skillfully, and the imperative that we not waste—all of these introduce us to the Bible's consistent witness on creation's behalf. Connecting these interpretations directly to environmental issues is still new to most people of faith, and to their clergy.

But there is more. More passages whose ecological significance faith communities are discovering. More eco-biblical themes for our new age. The next several decades will see the continued creation and proliferation of biblical interpretations related to the earth, and our treatment of it. Learning to read the Bible with "green" eyes represents one of the most exciting development in Biblical studies of the new millennium.

Several years ago, I was preaching in an urban congregation when Psalm 84 was read. I had never read this psalm while thinking about the environment, and the third verse, excerpted above, jumped off the page at me—"the sparrow too has found a home there; / the swallow has found herself a nest / where she can lay her young beside your altars, / LORD."

I've been around many, many worship spaces, many sanctuaries. I've watched hundreds of volunteers take great care cleaning the altar or holy table, making sure that the pulpit or *bima* is beautified for worship. I don't know what any of these volunteers would have reacted if they'd found a sparrow's nest at the side of the altar or atop the pulpit. Surprised? Upset? Puzzled?

And yet, Psalm 84 describes the sparrow finding a home, the swallow a place where she can build a nest for her newborns. The altar, the place that symbolizes God drawing close to people, is flanked by a bird's nest. The Bible speaks with a surprising tenderness and love about the environment. It's our job to make sure that our treatment of the earth can be characterized by that same tenderness and care.

No One Else

There is a midrash, a Rabbinic commentary on the Bible, which goes as follows: "When God created the first human beings, God led them around the Garden of Eden and said: "Look at my works! See how beautiful they are—how excellent! For your sake I created them all. See to it that you do not spoil and destroy My world; for if you do, there will be no one else to repair it."[9]

Beauty and excellence. Protection and care. Accountability. This midrash sums up many of this chapter's themes. May we be inspired to listen, and to act accordingly.

The Bible and the Earth

Here are a couple of exercises that can help small groups in congregations connect their knowledge of the Bible with their commitment to being good environmental stewards.

Your Own Private Eco-Bible

Each individual in the group should review the passages cited in this chapter, or other biblical passages that he or she knows, and connect them to the environment. Select two passages, and write down a two- to three-sentence description of what the passage means to you, why it is important to you about the environment. Then, take turns sharing these passages and the themes that they express. Are there similar or related themes between the passages that different group members have selected? What are these? What do members of the group learn from hearing one another's selections and interpretations?

Discussion Questions

1. Think of a spiritual experience you've had outdoors. Then, think about the biblical themes on the environment described in this chapter—themes of God's ownership, our awe and humility, our power and responsibility, and the wider community that includes all of creation. Does your own experience reflect or correspond with any of these biblical themes, or with a specific biblical passage? Take turns sharing your experiences, biblical themes, or passages that you associate with them.

2. Imagine that you've been given the assignment of writing an updated version of the biblical creation story. Members of the group should take five minutes and write down as much of their own version of this story as they can. Then, take turns reading the different versions of these stories aloud. What themes do each of these stories emphasize? Why?

Chapter 3

For the Bible Tells Me So

The New Testament and Nature's Protection

Ask a child to point to where God lives and you'll get a definitive response. Up.

I've asked thousands of children this question during children's sermons or religious education classes at congregations. If you ask a group of children where God lives, ninety-five out of one hundred will immediately point up. No hesitation. No question. Remarkable certainty. For the vast majority of kids, it's a given that God is up.

And the remaining 5 percent? Mostly, they point in toward their own heart. I like that. It suggests that their religious education or Sunday school teachers have a sense that God is with us, even within us, and not just up in the sky.

But I have never, not once, seen a single child point down toward the ground, toward the Earth, when asked where God lives. Nor have I seen a child point horizontally, or arc a crooked finger around them to indicate God's omnipresence. When it comes to knowing where God lives, children are certain.

God lives up in the sky. Away from the Earth.

I think it's likely that some children get this sense of where God lives from parents who face the painful task of comforting a child in the wake of the death of a beloved relative, or of a pet. "Where is Granny?" a child asks. Or Grandpa. Or the family dog who has died of old age. "With God in heaven," the parent replies. "Where is heaven?" asks the child. Most parents, at that point, don't really know what to say. Pointing up is still the default response for many, as unsatisfying a response as that might be.

Up, Up, and Away

This sense that God lives up there translates powerfully but problematically into adulthood. Most Christian adults, if asked about how the Bible ends and about the ultimate fate of the Earth, give an answer like this. "At the end of time, when the Day of Judgment comes, Jesus will return from heaven, gather up all the Christians, and somehow beam them up to the sky, where they meet God. After this evacuation is complete, God will blow up the Earth, destroying the planet and everyone who's not Christian. Jesus and the Christians will then take off into deep space, where God lives."

While this may seem like a crude summary of the plot line at the end of the New Testament, it will ring true to most people. For our purposes, this story has a clear physical direction. It's up. The unmistakable implication of this understanding of the story is that God lives "up there," away from the Earth. That when God finally acts to bring judgment and justice to their fullness, God crushes the earth with unmatched force, pulverizing it as a sign of divine righteousness. This story couldn't be less friendly to the environment, and less supportive to an ethic of care for creation. It makes it unequivocally clear that the direction of salvation—up, up, and away—demonstrates that, to God, the Earth ultimately doesn't matter. And it also opens the door to the question that follows logically. If the Earth doesn't matter to God, why should it matter to us?

Different Strokes for Different Folks

Christians from varying theological backgrounds treat this story very differently.

I'm Not Listening

Theologically liberal and moderate Christians aren't comfortable with this ending to the Bible. So, they ignore it. They feel that this part of the New Testament is violent, tribal, and embarrassing, that it shows God in a destructive and hateful light. They're befuddled by the imagery of God yanking Christians en masse off the face of the Earth, like a large scale medi-vac operation or a mass beam-up out of *Star Trek*. In the face of these interpretive hurdles, they abandon the end of the New Testament because they don't think it represents good news. Confusing news, or repulsive news, maybe. But not good.

Bring It On

Theologically conservative or fundamentalist Christians, on the other hand, often like this part of the Bible, and talk about it a lot. They believe that this end to the Bible shows that God matters, that our choices—of right and wrong, of whom and what we worship—have consequences. That God has a plan for us beyond this planet, beyond this life. For these Christians, this story is a validation, an affirmation of the commitments they've made and the beliefs they've embraced. It confirms that God is faithful, that right will win out over wrong, that our faith and hope can be trusted.

Let's Go to the Videotape

When I was growing up, there was a well-known New York area sportscaster named Warner Wolf. Wolf's signature line was, "Let's go to the videotape." It was his segue into looking at clips from different sporting events, telling the story of the various games he covered by looking at the source material of his trade—the highlight reel.

When it comes to the New Testament story of the second coming, if the source material is the Bible itself, there's one thing that liberal, moderate, and conservative Christians have in common. Not enough of them spend much time examining what the New Testament actually says, actually teaches about Jesus's relationship with or attitude toward the earth or the second coming. In the vast majority of churches, there's been no examination of the actual biblical witness in this area. Nobody's looking at the "videotape," the biblical text itself.

That's what we're going to do.

What Would Jesus Do?

Before jumping right to a discussion of the second coming and the Earth, though, let's pause and ask a first question: What was Jesus's relationship with the Earth like? What role did it play in his life? What key themes can we glean from reading the Gospels? And how did the early church, as evidenced in Paul's letters, view Jesus, his death and resurrection, in relation to the Earth? Let's start with the gospels' witness on the actual life of Jesus, and then see what the earliest churches had to say.

Head for the Hills

On many occasions, when Jesus was stressed or overburdened, when he needed to reflect and to pray, to reconnect with the source of his identity and strength, he did the same thing, over and over.

He headed for the hills.

Consider these three passages, from among many similar ones.

When he sent [his disciples] away, he went up onto a mountain by himself to pray. (Matt 14:23)

During that time, Jesus went out to the mountain to pray, and he prayed to God all night long. (Luke 6:12)

Early in the morning, well before sunrise, Jesus rose and went to a deserted place where he could be alone in prayer. (Mark 1:35)

Jesus's actions speak volumes about his connection to creation. They echo the themes of awe and wonder that we explored earlier, an awe that is the common birthright of all people—even the Son of God. Over and over, when Jesus needed spiritual revitalization, he knew where he wanted to go. Not to an organized religious institution or the town square, though these are both important. He went outdoors.

Teach-In or Teach-Out?

Now when Jesus saw the crowds, he went up a mountain. He sat down and his disciples came to him. He taught them, saying: "Happy are people who are hopeless, because the kingdom of heaven is theirs."

—Matthew 5:1-3

Teaching was a central part of Jesus's ministry. Among his teachings, none was more significant than the Sermon on the Mount. Referred to by some as "the Magna Carta of Christianity," its priority is clear.

But very few people pay attention to where Jesus chose to deliver this address. Again—he didn't choose a town square or a religious institution. He chose a mountain, a place of natural awe. And he took his closest followers there to form them, shape them with the depths of his message.

Jesus didn't only find rejuvenation for himself outdoors. He chose the outdoors as a place to initiate his followers into his worldview. His reality. God's reality.

Peak Experience

Six days later, Jesus took Peter, James, and John and brought them to the top of a very high mountain where they were alone. He was transformed in front of them, and his clothes were amazingly bright, brighter than if they had been bleached white.

—Mark 9:2-3

If the Sermon on the Mount represents a pinnacle of Jesus's teachings, the transfiguration represents an apex of his self-revelation as the Christ. Apart from the cross and resurrection, few gospel stories speak more compellingly about Jesus's identity.

Where did the transfiguration happen? "The top of a very high mountain." It was, literally, a peak experience.

We can see from these texts that Jesus valued the outdoors as a place to pray, to find out his true identity. He recognized the power of nature to open people to the depths of wisdom about God. He knew that exposure to nature enabled people to see the divine more directly. In other words, he got it. He understood and valued the creation as a place of tremendous spiritual significance, a place of divine revelation, a place where people became more open to the world of the Spirit.

Cursing the Tree?

Some Christians refer to the story of Jesus cursing the fig tree (see Mark 11, Matt 21) as suggesting that Jesus harbored antipathy for the natural world. There's absolutely nothing in the Gospels or in their depiction of Jesus's character that would support such an interpretation. Most commentators have interpreted this story as representing an assertion of Jesus's power over nature, as in his stilling of the storm or walking on water. Others see this passage as a metaphor in which Jesus's cursing the tree represented God's judgment on those who appear successful but who fail to live fruitfully (sorry—it's hard to resist the pun in this case). Without choosing between these interpretations, it's more than fair to say that there's no basis for understanding this story as revealing Jesus's hidden animus toward the Earth.

For the Birds

There's another familiar story in which Jesus says that God watches over the "birds in the sky" who "don't sow seed or harvest grain or gather crops into barns. Yet your heavenly Father feeds them. Aren't you worth much more than they are?" (Matt 6:26). As with the fig tree, some have interpreted Jesus's statement as an implicit devaluing of nature. Again, this is misguided. First, this passage is part of a longer passage in which Jesus talks about the danger of anxiety and excessive worry. Denigrating nature is simply not part of this passage's intent. Second, the passage asserts God's care and commitment to feeding the "birds in the sky," an affirmation of their value. Third, and perhaps most convincingly, after speaking about the birds, Jesus proceeds to talk about the lilies of the field, describing their beauty as follows: "They don't wear themselves out with work, and they don't spin cloth. But I say to you that even Solomon in all of his splendor wasn't dressed like one of these" (Matt 6:28-29).

If Jesus appeared to favor people over birds in the first part of this passage, then he seems to value flowers over a king in the second part of the same passage.

Ultimately, using the Bible to try to settle a picayune arguing about who is more important—birds or flowers or people—is a fruitless waste of time. The Gospels are clear that Jesus valued the natural world as a source of spiritual sustenance and support, that he used the natural world as a context and setting for some of his most energizing teaching, and that his true identity was revealed to his disciples in places of natural power. When it comes to Jesus's relationship to nature, and the value he placed on it, the verdict couldn't be clearer.

Salvation for the Universe

Let's look now at the ways in which early Christian writers viewed Jesus Christ's relationship with the Earth and the universe. Let's examine their perspective not just on the human Jesus's relationship with the planet but on the Son of God's relationship to the entire universe.

Cosmic Christ

In the letter to the Colossians, we find the following stunningly beautiful image of Christ, in the form of a hymn. It's intended to be sung, poetic praise of the highest order.

> *The Son is the image of the invisible God,*
> *the one who is first over all creation,*
>
> *Because all things were created by him:*
> *both in the heavens and on the earth,*
> *the things that are visible and the things that are invisible.*
> *Whether they are thrones or powers,*
> *or rulers or authorities,*
> *all things were created through him and for him.*
>
> *He existed before all things,*
> *and all things are held together in him.*
>
> *He is the head of the body, the church,*
> *who is the beginning,*
> *the one who is firstborn from among the dead*
> *so that he might occupy the first place in everything.*

Because all the fullness of God was pleased to live in him,
and he reconciled all things to himself through him—
whether things on earth or in the heavens.
He brought peace through the blood of his cross.

—Colossians 1:15-20

Two themes are notable here. First, Christ is a mystical presence that pervades everything and that holds everything together. Christ is the force that enables the universe to cohere, to exist, to make sense. Second, the scope of Christ's resurrection is not focused solely on Christians, or even on people. It is truly universal. The entire created order, "all things . . . whether things on earth or in the heavens," are reconciled to God, made whole by the power of Christ's death and new birth.

Again, the tone of the relationship between Christ and creation is loving, positive, and saving. Not dismissive. Not destructive. Not derogatory. There is respectful continuity between the relationship of the earthly Jesus and the resurrected Christ with the Earth. And there's an energizing beauty implicit in this early Christian expression of praise.

For God So Loved...What?

God so loved the world....

—John 3:16

This passage, one of the best known in the entire New Testament, is often used as a summation of the promise of salvation to those who believe in Christ. But once again, if one looks more closely, there's a compelling recognition that the scope of Christ's salvation is wider than we normally believe. Read the verse again.

It does not say, "For God so loved Christians."

It does not say, "For God so loved human beings."

It says, "For God so loved the world." The Greek word translated as "world"—*kosmos*—means "universe," the created order. This statement, a favorite of Evangelical Christians who affirm the priority that Christ represents, itself represents an affirmation of God's love for the earth and everything else.

What Kind of Flesh?

The Word became flesh
and made his home among us.
We have seen his glory,

glory like that of a father's only son,
full of grace and truth.

—John 1:14

This same theme, that the scope of Christ's salvation includes the creation and the community of life, appears in another well-known passage from John's Gospel. In this early Christian hymn, the author describes Christ, God's Word, becoming flesh and dwelling among us. The assumption that most people make is that the "flesh" in question is human flesh, and infer from this a human focus of Christ's work. The aim of the church, then, is to extend Christ's love to all people.

This reading of the text is incomplete. Biblical Greek has two words for flesh. One of these words, *anthropos*, means specifically human flesh, human life. The second word, *sarx*, refers to the flesh of all living beings. Which word did the author choose? *Sarx.* The flesh with which Christ adorned himself, the flesh which Christ ultimately redeemed, was not only human flesh, but rather the flesh of all living beings. Though not explicitly cosmic in its scope, this verse reinforces the clear arc of meaning that we've seen repeatedly. The scope, the reach, the impact of Christ's death and resurrection is broader, larger, deeper than Christians normally comprehend. It includes all living beings, not just us.

The End of the End of the World

Now, let's return to the question of the second coming, the end of time, the Final Judgment. The time that is supposedly bad news for the earth. As the sportscaster said, let's "go to the videotape"—or in this case, the Bible.

In its early decades, the Christian movement lived with the expectation that the second coming was real and imminent. It wasn't an abstraction. It was a source of hope, an anticipated event that impinged on peoples' values and behavior. And the leaders of the early church, such as Paul, tried hard to understand it, given their faith and their hope for what they believed God was going to do.

Downwardly Mobile

Paul's First Letter to the Thessalonians, written in the year 52 CE, is chronologically the earliest book in the New Testament. Paul wrote to offer encouragement to the members of the church in Thessalonica, urging them to persevere as they awaited the second coming of Christ. Understandably, people were curious about what the second coming would be like. Paul, never shy about speaking his beliefs, offered a description that became a foundation for later interpretations of this event. Here's how he described it.

Brothers and sisters, we want you to know about people who have died so that you won't mourn like others who don't have any hope. Since we believe that Jesus died and rose, so we also believe that God will bring with him those who have died in Jesus. What we are saying is a message from the Lord: we who are alive and still around at the Lord's coming definitely won't go ahead of those who have died. This is because the Lord himself will come down from heaven with the signal of a shout by the head angel and a blast on God's trumpet. First, those who are dead in Christ will rise. Then, we who are living and still around will be taken up together with them in the clouds to meet with the Lord in the air. That way we will always be with the Lord. (1 Thess 4:13-17)

Let's look at what this passage actually says. In the years following Jesus's resurrection, early Christians believed that his return was imminent, that they would see it within their lifetimes. By the time that Paul was writing this letter, some of those earliest Christians had died, and people were wondering what would happen to those who had died when the second coming finally took place. Paul is responding to this question. With endearing confidence, Paul tells them that when Jesus returns, the "dead in Christ" will rise first. Then, those Christians who are living will be "taken up in the clouds with them to meet with the Lord in the air. That way we will always be with the Lord." The image that this evokes for most people is something out of science fiction. Imagine the *Star Trek* mass beam-up that I mentioned earlier—thousands of people, mysteriously, ascending to the clouds where they meet with Jesus, who has descended from God's true home, way up in the sky. Once they've met Jesus in the clouds, it's a short step to imagining that Jesus and his band of believers will take off into deep space while God, eager to finish the job, detonates the heavenly weapon of mass destruction, finishing off the Earth and everything left behind. At first glance, this passage seems to confirm the aforementioned view of God as itching to "off" the earth, eager for a planetary Armageddon.

But if we look more closely at this passage, a different view appears. The Greek verb translated "to meet with the Lord in the air"—*apateson*—appears elsewhere in the New Testament with a very clear meaning. The word appears in the book of Acts (28:15) to describe how members of the early church in Rome walked forty-three miles out from the center of Rome to meet with Paul as he arrived for a visit. Forty-three miles! I can guarantee you that these early Christians did not walk that distance simply to greet Paul and then to walk away from Rome with him. Exactly the opposite. They went out to greet him, to welcome him to Rome as an honored guest. This same verb appears with the same meaning in non-biblical Greek literature of the same era. The word *apateson* means, "to welcome or greet a visiting dignitary or person of importance."

Viewed in this way, the description in the First Letter to the Thessalonians doesn't mean that Jesus has returned to whisk Christians away from the earth before God finishes it off. It means that at the second coming, Paul envisioned a joyous group, which mysteriously includes the living and the dead, welcoming Jesus back to the earth. Jesus is returning not to inaugurate a grand departure or abandonment of the planet, but to bring the Earth to its fullness of being, its intended glory, in a way that only God can do. The direction of salvation is not up, up, and away. It's toward the earth, toward an ultimate healing, restoration, and reckoning that makes everything right.

Let's look at some further passages that reinforce this "downwardly mobile" view of the direction of salvation.

Left Behind

Almost everyone has heard of the Left Behind series of books, a set of fictional novels that describe the struggles of a small band of Christians against a godless, evil set of opponents in the overall context of the approach of the second coming. It's fair to say that for the characters in this series, you do not want to be "left behind." Consistent with the earth-destructive beliefs described earlier, the premise of this bestselling series is that after the faithful have been evacuated from the earth and made their way to the far reaches of space where God lives, God will destroy the earth and everyone and everything that's, well, left behind.

The phrase "left behind" is a biblical phrase that appears in the Gospels of Matthew and Luke (though contemporary translators often say "left" instead of "left behind"). Here's the passage from Matthew.

> But nobody knows when that day or hour will come, not the heavenly angels and not the Son. Only the Father knows. As it was in the time of Noah, so it will be at the coming of the Human One. In those days before the flood, people were eating and drinking, marrying and giving in marriage, until the day Noah entered the ark. They didn't know what was happening until the flood came and swept them all away. The coming of the Human One will be like that. At that time there will be two men in the field. One will be taken and the other left. Two women will be grinding at the mill. One will be taken and the other left. Therefore, stay alert! (Matt 24:36-42)

This passage is part of a longer speech that Jesus gives to describe the second coming. The common understanding of this specific passage is that it's bad to be left behind. But again, a careful reading reveals the opposite. The passage begins with the example of Noah, in which Noah, his family, and the animals were saved—left behind—while the flood swept everyone else away. This sets up the proper interpretive scheme for this passage. To be swept away is bad. To be left behind is good. It means that you are safe, protected from harm.

The passage then proceeds to give several examples of what the second coming will be like. Two men will be working. One will be taken, another left behind. The same for two women grinding wheat, an everyday task. One taken, one left. If one follows the logic of the passage, left behind is where you want to be. It's being swept away, taken away, that's the problem.

Paradise—Here!

Each year, the Sierra Club, one of the country's leading environmental organizations, publishes a gorgeous calendar. The monthly version has twelve beautiful nature pictures, photos of mountains and plains, trees and rivers, mammals, birds, and more. It's a nature lover's paradise. The weekly version does the same thing, but has fifty-two of these images, one per week. It's almost too much beauty for one publication.

But there's something missing. People. None of the photos, ever, includes a human person. It's wall-to-wall nature. Apart from the fact that a person took the photo him or herself, you couldn't guess that people even existed.

The New Testament has its own, different image of paradise, and it's found at the end of the book of Revelation. This book is one of the most challenging of any in the Bible. But when it comes to the fate of the earth and the direction of our salvation, its message is clear. Let's review a few passages toward the end of Revelation, where the author describes paradise from a Christian perspective.

New Heaven, New Earth?

> *Then I saw a new heaven and a new earth, for the former heaven and the former earth had passed away, and the sea was no more. I saw the holy city, New Jerusalem, coming down out of heaven from God, made ready as a bride beautifully dressed for her husband. I heard a loud voice from the throne say, "Look! God's dwelling is here with humankind. He will dwell with them, and they will be his peoples. God himself will be with them as their God. He will wipe away every tear from their eyes. Death will be no more. There will be no mourning, crying, or pain anymore, for the former things have passed away.*

—Revelation 21:1-4

I know who made the environment. He's coming back and he's going to burn it all up.
So yes, I drive an SUV. [1]

—Pastor Mark Driscoll, Evangelical Pastor

49

This passage from Revelation offers an initial image of paradise, a Christian image of what heaven is like. Given our examination of this topic to date, three things jump out.

First, paradise is called "the New Jerusalem." It is a city, unlike the photos in the Sierra Club calendar. It affirms the value of people. We'll look at this dimension of Christianity's paradise in a moment.

Second, note the direction in which paradise is moving. It's not up, up, and away. Rather, the New Jerusalem is "coming down out of heaven." Once again, one of this chapter's main themes is reinforced. The second coming, the end of time, is not an escape from the earth, but rather Christ's return and God's recommitment to it. God's home is with us, here.

Third, the passage describes paradise as involving a "new heaven and a new earth." This passage has been used by many, such as the well-known pastor quoted above, to suggest that the second coming involves the wholesale destruction of the planet, the theme mentioned frequently in this chapter. After earth is wiped out, the reasoning goes, God will create an entirely new planet in its place.

The proper interpretation of this phrase, once again, depends on the meaning of the biblical Greek. There are two biblical Greek words for "new." One of these, *neos,* means brand new, newly made. The other, *kainos,* means renewed, rejuvenated. So, which word is used when referring to a "new heaven and a new earth"?

Kainos. A renewed heaven, and a renewed Earth.

Revelation's vision isn't an endorsement of a "torched" mind-set. It's a confirmation that God's commitment to the Earth is every bit as real, every bit as long-lasting, as God's commitment to us.

What Kind of Paradise?

> *Then the angel showed me the river of life-giving water, shining like crystal, flowing from the throne of God and the Lamb through the middle of the city's main street. On each side of the river is the tree of life, which produces twelve crops of fruit, bearing its fruit each month. The tree's leaves are for the healing of the nations.*
>
> —Revelation 22:1-2

As noted above, the New Testament's vision of paradise is a city, the New Jerusalem. In ancient times, the city was the height of human achievement, the center of human commerce and governance. Jerusalem in particular was the city of the temple, the place that embodied God's commitment and closeness to the people of Israel.

But Revelation's New Jerusalem isn't an ordinary city. From the passage above, one can see that it is a city with a life-giving river flowing down its main avenue, an avenue bordered by fruit-bearing trees. This is a paradise in which human achievement and nature are beautifully and deeply intertwined, seamlessly integrated. Nature and people aren't opposed or at odds; they coexist peacefully. And the statement that "the tree's leaves are for the healing of the nations" suggests that human society, represented by "the nations," is ultimately dependent on the natural world for its sustenance and healing.

The New Testament's vision of paradise is one in which people and planet live together in well-being, joined in God's collective embrace.

My Body, My Blood

While they were eating, Jesus took bread, blessed it, broke it, and gave it to the disciples and said, "Take and eat. This is my body." He took a cup, gave thanks, and gave it to them, saying, "Drink from this, all of you. This is my blood of the covenant, which is poured out for many so that their sins may be forgiven."

—Matthew 26:26-28

There's a final passage that we'll consider before concluding. The passage above, well known to Christians, is the story of the Last Supper, the final meal Jesus ate before his arrest and eventual execution. At this meal, he took bread and wine, blessed them, asserted that they were his body and blood, and shared them with his disciples.

Jesus's statements, "This is my body" and "this is my blood" are statements of identification, assertions in which he equates bread and wine with his very self. So what is bread? It is wheat combined with human labor. Similarly, wine is a combination of grapes and human effort.

Theologians across the Christian spectrum have noted that these two statements of Jesus implicitly affirm the dignity of human labor. Pastor Dan Neary of Pleasant View Church offers an example of this reasoning. "In order for this Holy moment to take place, Jesus had to rely on the skill and labor of others. Skilled farmers had to produce the wheat and the grapes. Others had to prepare the raw ingredients, skillfully storing them and perhaps transporting them. And yet others had to apply the crafts they had learned, likely passed down through generations and practiced for years before perfected. Countless skilled hands, and hours of labor, were represented as Jesus took the bread and the cup in His hands."[2]

Catholic Social Teaching sounds similar themes. Because they involve human labor, the bread and wine that Jesus dignifies in the Last Supper implicitly dignify human work.

This reasoning leads to a related conclusion. If labor, one of the ingredients required to make bread and wine, is dignified, then why not the other ingredient? Why not the wheat and the grapes, the fruits of the earth, and by extension the earth itself?

The time has arrived for Christianity to recognize creation's basic dignity alongside humanity's. This doesn't mean that creation is perfect; we don't make that claim for people either. But it does mean that it is wrong to act in a way that persistently and systematically degrades and destroys creation, whose dignity represents nothing more than its God-given status.

When we began our exploration of the Bible's teachings on the environment, one of the first passages we explored was Genesis 1, in which God repeatedly affirmed creation's inherent value, it's divinely ordained merit, worth, and goodness. It's fitting that our exploration of the Bible's teachings on the earth concludes with this same theme.

The New Testament witness is consistent and clear. The natural world is a place where we meet God, are empowered to know God, see God more clearly than many other places. God values creation with the same ultimacy with which God values us, and God has imbued creation with the same dignity with which we ourselves have been invested. From the New Testament's perspective, the fate of the earth is the same as our fate. We are both, all, loved, healed, restored, and redeemed by God.

Discussion Questions

1. When Jesus needed to reconnect with God, he went outdoors to pray. Have you ever gone outdoors to pray, or to reconnect with God? Share stories of times when you've done this.

2. This chapter begins with the assertion that most people think God lives "up"—away from the Earth. What would it be like to affirm that God's home is "down here" on the Earth? What difference would that make to your faith?

3. This chapter offers a different interpretation of the second coming than most Christians have learned. In your group, discuss the understandings of the second coming that you've held in the past. What were the positive aspects of this understanding? The negative aspects? What is your reaction to this "downwardly mobile" interpretation of the second coming?

Chapter 4

Many Faiths, One Earth

Eco-Teachings from the World's Religions

An Overview of Diverse Teachings on the Environment

In the last two chapters, we've reviewed environmental teachings from the Bible, sampling Jewish and Christian wisdom in relation to the earth. Of the world's overall population of seven billion people, approximately a third, or 2.2 billion, are Christian. Another fifteen million are Jews. This leaves almost five billion other people, over 65 percent of the population.

Following Christianity, Islam is the world's second largest religion by number of adherents, with 1.6 billion followers, or 23 percent of the world's population. About 1.1 billion people consider themselves religiously unaffiliated, making this the third largest group on the planet. These "nones" are followed closely by Hindus (one billion, 15 percent), Buddhists (five hundred million, 7 percent), and 460 million people (just under 7 percent) who practice indigenous traditions such as African traditional religions, Chinese folk religions, Native American religions, or Australian aboriginal religions, or who identify with the Baha'i, Jain, Sikh, Shinto, Taoist, Tenrikyo, Unitarian Universalist, Wicca, or Zoroastrianism traditions.[1]

The world is a religiously diverse place, and we're going to take a short tour of the teachings on the environment from a number of religions. As the United States becomes more spiritually diverse, there are three reasons that there's value in such a tour. First, as religious diversity becomes a norm rather than an exception, awareness of diverse moral teachings gives us a rich collection of ideas from which we can draw to create an environmentally sustainable society. The world's religions have different, yet interestingly related worldviews that give rise to environmental values that are sometimes similar, sometimes different, and sometimes differently emphasized. In a pluralistic world, we need this kind of rich collection of values from various sources, a multi-dimensional conceptual toolbox from which we can draw to protect the earth.

Second, by promoting mutual understanding, interfaith awareness strengthens relations between different cultural and religious communities who too easily misunderstand one another.

Third, learning about traditions and teachings that are different from our own forces us to think, to learn, to examine our own deep assumptions about our faith and about the earth. It gives us the chance to reexplore our own beliefs, to have these beliefs challenged and strengthened, and to grow in the process. Rather than undermining or weakening our faith, whatever that faith may be and however it may be expressed, this process of inquiry ultimately deepens and strengthens belief. It may also change it, and force it to evolve. This can be threatening and frightening, but it is a vital part of having a living faith. Faith that does not grow, if not in its essentials then in the way in which those essentials are interpreted and applied to life, quickly becomes an empty shell. There is no such thing as a static spirituality. People go through different stages of life. Cultures face new, unanticipated challenges. New ways of believing, new applications of timeless teachings, are necessary for survival.

So, to understand an introductory range of religious teachings on the environment is to be a religiously engaged person, seeking to discern a faithful response to one of the great challenges that faces us. And this broader understanding helps us build relationships with our neighbors, colleagues, and friends from different cultures and traditions. It enables us to search together more effectively, more meaningfully, for common ground in relation to our common home.

Around the World

In this chapter, I'll start by offering a brief overview of environmental teachings from the religious traditions of First Peoples, indigenous peoples, from around the world. I'll follow this with wisdom from Hinduism and Buddhism, then teachings from Confucianism and Taoism, the major religious influences on China, and conclude with an overview of Islamic teachings on the earth. This overview is not intended to be exhaustive. And because I write as a Christian, I apologize in advance for the ways in which my own background will cause me to interpret others' traditions in either a tone deaf or insensitive way.

I'll be featuring the strongest environmental teachings from each tradition. But it's not my intention to idealize these traditions, any more than I meant to idealize Judaism and Christianity in the previous two chapters. No tradition is perfectly "green," in theory or in practice. Rather, my intent is to offer up some of the best ideas, the most valuable beliefs that these diverse traditions have articulated in relation to the earth. These beliefs can move and provoke us to take ecological concerns more seriously, to think about them more clearly, and to establish a stronger values-based foundation to support our response to the environmental crisis.

In the Beginning—Indigenous Religions and the Environment

Before there were world religions, "portable" faiths with a global scope such as Buddhism or Christianity or Islam, the peoples of the earth were gathered in tribes and clans, in local or regional societies that relied on their landscape and its non-human inhabitants—their bioregion—for physical sustenance, spiritual revelation, and religious meaning. These First Peoples' survival is under grave threat on a worldwide basis today, due to a range of cultural forces and pressures from governments and multinational corporations eager to control the natural resources that lie on or under native lands. But during their extraordinarily long residence in their specific bioregions, indigenous peoples have developed a remarkably close relationship with their beyond-human surroundings, a relationship with several themes that are valuable for our overview.

Indigenous peoples live around the world, in a large number of distinct geographic, ethnographic, and cultural settings. We must recognize that offering generalizations about these varied peoples runs the risk of disregarding and disrespecting their individuality. Respectful of this hazard, let's explore several themes central to the worldview, spirituality, and religion of the planet's First Peoples.

I Am This Place

In Huston Smith's classic book *The World's Religions,* Smith tells a story about a young Native American leader, one of the first in his tribe to go to college. Several members of his family were determined that he not lose his sense of Native American identity. On one of his first visits home, an elder took him in a canoe out onto a lake surrounded by forests, a landscape vital to the tribe's identity. In the middle of the lake, the elder stopped paddling and asked the young leader, over and over, "Who are you?" The young man cycled through a series of responses. "Child of my parents." "Member of this tribe." "Member of my generation." None of these satisfied the elder, who finally interrupted impatiently. "You are this lake. You are this water. You are these trees," he said, sternly. "Remember that."[2]

For many First Peoples, relationship with a specific place, a specific region is fundamental to their identity. Some have observed that if US citizens think of their own identity as stopping at the boundary of their own skin, that Native Peoples' identity has a much broader reach, and includes the place in which their people have lived, often for millennia. This is not an inconsequential reality for indigenous peoples. Evidence abounds that, when displaced from their home landscape, indigenous peoples suffer greatly. Losing their bioregional home is a traumatic dislocation that severely harms their well-being, individually and collectively.

This Place Is Sacred

But it doesn't stop there. An essential part of the life of indigenous peoples is the experience of the sacred in relation to specific natural places that contain spiritual power and convey divine wisdom in a way that transforms human life, enables people to mature from one stage of life, one level of consciousness, to the next. Indigenous peoples believe these sacred places hold the unique power to constitute their identity as members of their tribe. These places are not "transferable" or movable. They are the enduring "thin places" in which the membrane separating the realm of the divine from human life is porous and permeable. They are essential to the being of indigenous peoples. Without the energy and meaning they convey, indigenous people and their cultures disintegrate.

On occasions too numerous to recount, the world's indigenous peoples have been forcibly displaced from these homelands, dispossessed of access to the sacred places that make them who they are, with gravely dire effects. This displacement represents a horrific injustice. It is one of the greatest tragedies of the modern world, too infrequently recognized.

Living Universe, Extended Family

In addition to identifying profoundly with their home region, indigenous peoples see it as alive in many of its aspects and manifestations, as having consciousness, intentionality, and purpose. It is common for indigenous peoples to recognize some form of "personhood" in connection to the animals, plants, land, and weather of their native regions, and to have customs through which they acknowledge, manage, and maintain their relationships with these members of their extended family.

For example, John Grim, a leading scholar of indigenous "lifeways"[3] and the environment, writes that Native Peoples often recognize a collective identity of animals, such as "bird nation" or "deer peoples," evidence that they viewed these animals as being "peoples" who command respectful treatment or behavior, just as one would behave respectfully toward a human uncle or aunt. Grim further observes that indigenous peoples believe that plants, animals, and mineral spirits demonstrate "affection" for their tribe, an affection that these peoples return in the form of gifts offered to the land and its native plants and animals, or with various forms of self-restraint (e.g., refraining from hunting in a certain area during certain times of year).[4] Often, this restraint may have a practical as well as spiritual value. For example, if a tribe that depends on a certain animal for sustenance refrains from hunting during the animal's mating or young-bearing seasons, it is more likely that a healthy population of those animals will survive.

I find it admirable that these religious practices lead both to the protection of nature and the survival and flourishing of the human community. Good religion ought to help us survive, ought to promote well-being. There's nothing wrong with spirituality that supports abundant human life, a healthy relationship with the earth, and a sustainable balance between people and planet. In fact, I'd argue that this must become one of religion's main functions in our time.

For indigenous peoples, the natural world is a living community of persons, an extended kin network, which deserves love and respect that needs to be demonstrated both emotionally and concretely, physically. This sensibility, which one appreciates quickly when hearing Native Peoples speak about their homeland, could not be farther from the highly impersonal relationship with the land, the "geography of nowhere"[5] that characterizes so much of US life.

Sustainable Presence

Native Peoples' long identification with their specific bioregions, often over the course of thousands of years, gives rise to a place-based wisdom that is referred to as "traditional ecological knowledge." In other words, these Native Peoples have developed unique insights about living within their home region in a way that has proven truly sustainable in both human and ecological terms. The United Nations,[6] the World Bank,[7] and numerous anthropologists have recognized that the presence of a significant population of indigenous peoples frequently results in the protection of a notable degree of biodiversity. Leaders of these modern institutions have come to recognize what indigenous peoples have known for millennia—that a people's close relationship with a specific place can result in a manner of human presence that protects a wide range of life forms and that is sustainable over thousands of years.

This sustainable presence does not mean that indigenous peoples leave nature as untouched wilderness—far from it. Researchers such as Gary Paul Nabhan[8] have demonstrated that Native Peoples in the southwestern United States, for example, made significant modifications in their landscape to render it more hospitable for their habitation. The fact that Native Peoples made changes in their landscapes, however, should not be surprising. To be human is to impact the environment. What is remarkable is that the changes made have proven, in a number of cases, to be so sustainable not for decades or centuries, but for millennia.

Summary of Key Themes

To summarize, indigenous peoples often identify profoundly with the place or region where they have lived for centuries, or even millennia. Specific outdoor sacred sites play a fundamental role in the development of the essential character of the people, serving as the locations for rituals through which peoples' core selfhood, individually and collectively, is evoked and bestowed. Many indigenous peoples view the earth and the universe as living, endowed with consciousness, personhood, and purpose. Because the many members of the earth's wider community are viewed in this way, indigenous peoples believe that they owe a debt of respect, restraint, and gratitude to the landscapes and creatures that support their existence. And, because they have often lived in specific places for millennia, indigenous peoples possess a unique wisdom about how to live sustainably in their region, in a manner that supports a living balance between people and nature.

Surrounded by Divinity—Hindu Teachings on the Environment

Hinduism is the oldest continually practiced religion in the Indian subcontinent, and is certainly among the oldest religious traditions in the world. Scholars date its history from approximately 1500 BCE, the beginning of the period when the Vedas, the first Hindu sacred texts, were written. But rather than denoting a highly unified religion, *Hinduism* is a term that refers to the indigenous religions of India. Hinduism, really, is a collection of traditions that are related both geographically and thematically, not a centralized, single tradition of its own.

Hinduism has a rich set of teachings that are remarkably eco-friendly. These teachings represent a vitally important asset for the world's environment.

Divinity Every Which Way

One of Hinduism's core teachings is that the supreme and universal Spirit, referred to as *Brahman,* is understood to be the essence, the "heart and soul," of everything that is—all matter, time, and space. The Sanskrit phrase *Vasudeva Sarvam* means "The Supreme Being resides in all things," a restatement of this basic tenet. Hindu leaders affirm the ecological significance of this belief, noting that if the essence of all is divine, then all of reality deserves to be treated with reverence. This basic teaching is a foundation of Hindu ecological thought.

Hinduism also enthusiastically embraces the idea that there are many, many manifestations of the divine—many *deva* (gods) and *devi* (goddesses). These deities take many forms, including but not limited to natural features such as mountains and rivers. The Ganges River, for example, is considered a deity by Hindus, who believe that bathing in her waters washes away sins and helps liberate the believer from an endless cycle of life, death, and rebirth. The Himalayan Mountains are another example of a deified natural feature, as is Mother Earth herself. One of the most widely known Hindu prayers is one that millions of Hindus say to *Bhumi*, Mother Earth, each morning upon awaking and before stepping out of bed. In addition to offering praise to *Bhumi*, the prayer asks forgiveness for treading on her.

Salutations to You, Oh Mother Earth! Who is decked by ocean as the garment
and mountains as the breasts! Kindly pardon me as I touch you by my feet[9]

—Hindu prayer

One of Hinduism's great beauties is its enthusiasm for recognizing the divine in many, many forms. This exuberance is foreign and off-putting to some monotheists, some of whom anxiously accuse Hindus of polytheism. This criticism misses the point. Hindus see one essential divinity in many forms, each form representing *Brahman* in various guises.

To be clear, Hinduism's designation of the earth, the Ganges, and other natural features as deities has not consistently translated into an ethic of care for the environment. Still, the high value that this tradition places on the earth represents an important cornerstone for a Hindu environmental ethic.

It's All Connected

The interconnectedness of all reality is another central Hindu theme with environmental significance. The Upanishads, one if the most highly respected Hindu sacred texts, describe the five elements that constitute all material reality flowing from *Brahman*, the godhead: "From *Brahman* arises space, from space arises air, from air arises fire, from fire arises water, and from water arises Earth."[10] If everything comes from some combination of these elements, each with their origin in *Brahman*, then all is interrelated, interconnected. These five elements even represent the material form of our bodies, notes Dr. Pankaj Jain, a leading scholar of Indic religious teachings on the environment. "Nature and the environment are not outside us, not alien or hostile to us," he writes. "They are an inseparable part of our existence."[11]

As we'll see in an upcoming chapter, scientists have learned that the natural world is characterized by its thoroughgoing interconnectedness, with each part of nature impacting each other. Hinduism's embrace of reality's interconnectedness, which it shares with Buddhism, is a good fit for an ecological age.

Nature and Nirvana

For Hindus, *nirvana* signifies unity with *Brahman,* and the profound peace that this represents. It is, in some ways, an equivalent term to salvation. It represents ultimate blessedness. Interestingly, it comes from a root word that means "to extinguish or to blow out," as in "to blow out a candle." In keeping with the underlying meaning of its linguistic origin, Buddhism and Hinduism both understand *nirvana* to represent our liberation from the confines of our egos (the extinguishing of our limited selves), and our unification with a far greater reality.

A number of traditional Hindu concepts can be interpreted and formed into a story line that shows how care for the earth can help lead toward *nirvana.* I'll offer brief definitions of each of these concepts, followed by an example of how they can be utilized in support of an earth-friendly ethos.

- *Dharma* is translated variously as "moral duty," "universal law," or "behavior necessary to uphold the proper order of things." It is a foundational concept that denotes right or proper conduct in various situations.

- *Karma* is a Hindu term that describes the inescapable moral trajectory that is generated by every human act, and which determines our future.

- *Ahimsa,* or "nonviolence," was a Hindu teaching made famous by Gandhi, for whom it was an ethical cornerstone. Recognizing that all human life causes some violence (for example, we must eat to live, and for us to eat, life must be taken), Hindus are instructed to cause as little violence as possible.

- *Sunyasa* means renunciation or self-restraint. Comparable in certain ways to Christian asceticism, Hinduism teaches that by detaching from the world's material trappings, people can proceed toward liberation (see below). The ecological value of *sunyasa* lies in its implicit critique of consumerism, the belief that material consumption in itself can bring fulfillment.

- *Moksha* is Sanskrit for "liberation." Hinduism teaches that all people move through millions of cycles of birth, life, and rebirth—on the path to *moksha* and ultimately to *nirvana*—the extinguishing of the changeable human personality with the peace that comes from union with *Brahman*.

So, if *Brahman* resides at the heart of all things, then one's moral duty, one's *dharma*, must reflect a respect, a reverence for all things, including that natural world. By treating the natural world with respect, one earns beneficial *karma*. Hindus speak of earning such *karma* in part through *sunyasa* and *ahimsa* toward the environment through such practices as vegetarianism, through which the killing of sentient beings is avoided. Beneficial *karma* leads, eventually, to rebirth into a more advanced state of being, a step forward on the path toward *moksha* and *nirvana*.

Where's the Beef?

When it comes to food consumption, these Hindu teachings have a large, beneficial environmental impact. According to the Union of Concerned Scientists, producing a pound of beef produces about eighteen times the greenhouse gas emissions as producing a pound of pasta. An average US family of four that cut its meat consumption in half could reduce its carbon footprint—the amount of CO_2 emissions that its consumption produces—by three tons annually.[12] Clearly, a diet that's low in meat consumption has significant environmental benefits.

Hinduism has traditionally advocated for a vegetarian diet, arguing that to earn good *karma*, we should practice nonviolence, *ahimsa*, in relation to other sentient life forms. In part as a result, various surveys put the percentage of the Indian population that is vegetarian at 30 to 40 percent, between 360 and 480 million people (The entire US population is approximately 315 million.). The UN's Food and Agriculture Organization reported in 2012 that of the world's 177 countries, Indian per capita meat consumption was lowest, at just over seven pounds per year. This compares to the US average of just over 275 pounds, the Brazilian average of just over 177 pounds, and the Chinese average of just over 119 pounds.[13] Clearly, some of India's low level of meat consumption is due to poverty.[14] But religious and cultural traditions play a vital role. As India becomes wealthier, we must hope that these Hindu leaders are able to invest these traditional teachings with a new urgency, and offer Hinduism's affirmation of vegetarianism as a gift to the world.

The Original Tree Huggers

To be called a tree hugger today is not a compliment. However, few people understand the Hindu origin of this phrase. Let's close our overview of Hindu eco-teachings by learning how the term was born.

In the late 1400s, Guru Jambheshwar, a leader of the Bishnois people in northern India, established twenty-nine moral precepts to ensure his people's well-being. In several of these precepts, he urged the protection of the environment. He had observed that when large numbers of trees were cut down, soil quality was degraded, flooding increased, food production decreased, and people were impoverished. Consequently, one of Guru Jambheshwar's injunctions prohibited the cutting down of trees. Over time, this led to the Bishnois region enjoying large, healthy forests.

In 1730, a king from a neighboring region, in search of timber for his palace, sent soldiers to harvest timber from the Bishnois' forests. The Bishnois, led by a woman, blocked access to the forest and rejected the soldiers' suggestion that they bribe the logging party to go elsewhere. The soldiers approached the Bishnois, demanding that they step aside. The Bishnois women and men responded by encircling and hugging trees to prevent the logging. More than 360 Bishnois were slain before the soldiers relented.[15] Tree hugging was born as an act of courageous moral, values-based commitment.

Fast forward 250 years, to the early 1970s. In northern India, in the foothills of the Himalayas, deforestation was on the rise, bringing with it the same interconnected social and environmental ills that Guru Jambheshwar had witnessed five centuries before, though on a larger scale. When heavy rains came and without protective forests, entire villages were washed away along with the region's life-sustaining topsoil. Women suffered particular hardship as a result of the clear-cutting. Responsible for gathering food for their animals and the firewood needed for their household's cooking and warmth, they were forced to walk enormous distances each day simply to gather the fodder and kindling they needed to survive.

Even as the region, known as the Chipko region, became increasingly deforested, the Indian government awarded sizeable logging contracts to several companies. Drawing on the memory of the Bishnois, Chipko women villagers gathered in protest, hugging the trees like their Bishnois forebears to prevent the logging. Their protest proved successful, and women-led groups around India adopted the tree-hugging tactic. Eventually, the Indian government formed a committee to look into these issues, and found in favor of the Chipko women. This set further changes in motion. By connecting protection of the environment with the improvement of living conditions for the poor, the Chipko Movement inspired a new generation of Indians to take up the cause of environmental stewardship, previously criticized as a concern of the affluent West. From this generation emerged new leaders who have begun to develop water management, energy conservation, reforestation, and recycling projects across India. The UN Environment Programme reported that the Chipko Movement has launched a "a socio-economic revolution by winning control of their forest resources from the hands of a distant bureaucracy which is only concerned with the selling of forestland for making urban-oriented products."[16]

In 1987, the Chipko Movement won the prestigious Right Livelihood Award, referred to as the alternative Nobel Peace Prize. The Movement remains a powerful example of the impact that religious teachings can have on the well-being of people and the planet.

Summary of Key Themes

In summary, Hinduism emphasizes that the divine is omnipresent, that the essence of all matter is *Brahman* and is sacred. Hinduism marks this by enthusiastically recognizing many gods and goddesses, including a number of natural features and Mother Earth herself, as manifestations of the godhead. To develop the *karma* that will lead to *nirvana*, Hindus must practice nonviolence and restraint in relation to the Earth. Environmental care is an essential aspect of *dharma,* the righteous path that one must walk to gain enlightenment and liberation.

Be Still and Know—Buddhist Teachings on the Environment

Born in the sixth century BCE, Siddartha Gautama was a young, wealthy man who embarked on a spiritual quest. In his mid-thirties, he traveled to Bodh Gaya in northern India, to the forested banks of the Neranjana River. He seated himself under a Bodhi tree, and entered a state of deep concentration.

After many days and nights of meditation, a timeless instant arrived. Veils of ignorance were lifted from his mind. Siddartha became a fully enlightened being, a Buddha, an Awakened One.

And it happened outdoors.

The world's five hundred million Buddhists, who are concentrated across East Asia, follow the Buddha's teachings and practices. While Buddhism shares a number of the Hindu teachings described above, it offers and emphasizes its own particular methods and prescriptions to protect the planet.

Mind the Mind

Environmental issues pose difficult challenges, challenges that often engender feelings of anger, hopelessness, defensiveness, and futility. In the United States, environmental issues frequently become emotionally polarizing, and political eco-gridlock has become a norm in Washington, DC. Well aware of the human mind's tendency to become reactive and dysfunctional under stress, many Buddhist responses to the environment begin by encouraging meditation, or "mindfulness practice," in order to quiet the mind. One Buddhist environmental scholar has written that "Mindfulness builds capacity and calmness for approaching difficulty,"[17] a prerequisite for engaging challenges like the environment. This scholar teaches that by replacing "chaos with calmness" and enhancing our ability to focus fully on others, or on the matter at hand, Buddhist meditative practice equips us to deal with environmental challenges more effectively than we'd otherwise be able to. In support of meditation's value in this regard, the Dalai Lama has said, "Because we all share this planet Earth, we have to learn to live in harmony and peace with each other and with nature. This is not just a dream, but a necessity."[18]

For Buddhists, the practice of mindfulness, of stilling the mind, leads in several additional directions. One of these is toward the recognition, as in Hinduism, that all reality is profoundly interconnected. We'll turn there now.

Interbeing

> *Imagine a multidimensional spider's web in the early morning covered with dew drops. And every dew drop contains the reflection of all the other dew drops. And in each reflected dew drop, the reflections of all the other dew drops in that reflection. And so ad infinitum. That is the Buddhist conception of the universe.*[19]

—Alan Watts

In Buddhist thought, the terms "dependent co-arising" and "interbeing" describe the web of causes, forces, persons, and events that interrelate all that is, all that has been, and all that will be. Indra's Net is one commonly-used Buddhist image that refers to this interdependence. A net with a multifaceted jewel at every node, each jewel is reflected in the others, as each line of the net is attached to and influenced by all others. Tug at one string and all quiver. Cloud one jewel and all are reflected less vibrantly.

"Life is precious. It is everywhere, inside us and all around us; it has so many forms," writes the great Buddhist monk Thich Nhat Hanh.[20] Meditative practice leads us, Buddhists assert, to grasp the preciousness of life and the interconnectedness of reality, which in turn leads us to live in a manner that causes less harm, less violence *(ahimsa),* less suffering. As in Hinduism, the result of such a manner of life is better *karma,* quicker progress toward liberation and enlightenment.

Compassion: Interbeing in Action

> *Not harming life. Not taking what is not given. Not participating in abusive relations.*

Not speaking falsely. Not using intoxicating substances or behaviors. All of these have environmental implications for personal and social behavior.[21]

—Dr. Stephanie Kaza

One of the fruits of a meditative practice, and of recognizing reality's essential oneness, is compassion. And as Dr. Kaza's quote above makes clear, compassion and environmental well-being are deeply intertwined. This simple spiritual reality has vital consequences in a consumerist society. It reminds us that our dietary choices don't only impact our own taste buds and waistlines; they have environmental and humanitarian impacts. Our choice of transportation isn't just a matter of our own taste in automobiles; our car's gas mileage and tailpipe emissions impact the environment and human health. Buddhism teaches that meditation leads to awareness of reality's interconnectedness, which in turn leads to compassion, the path of the enlightened person.

I Consume, Therefore I Am?

Many people believe that happiness is getting what we desire or crave. Buddhists use the term *trishna*—thirst—to describe this phenomenon. It is universal. From a Buddhist perspective, the spiritual journey is a struggle with *trishna*, a seeking to understand it and to set limits on its inevitably overreaching nature.

From a Buddhist perspective, one could not develop a more *trishna*-inducing society than US consumerism has done, a society in which we are repeatedly urged to chase from one craving to another in search of fulfillment. There's no doubt that we're all grateful for a level of material well-being and for certain creature comforts, many of which have freed people from drudgery and mindlessly repetitive tasks. But consumerism goes far beyond that. Its bold, materialist claim is that consumption equals fulfillment, a clearly nonreligious assertion. Yet consumerism is an increasingly common view of the good life on a global level.

Advertisements, consumerism's lingua franca, are ubiquitous. Ads can now be found everywhere. A *New York Times* article on advertising reported that ads now show up on actual eggs in some supermarkets, where CBS has advertised some of its television shows (One eggshell, advertising a detective show, boasted that in a certain episode, the case would be "cracked"). Not to be outdone, many airlines sell ad space on their motion sickness bags. A person living in a US city today, according to a leading ad agency, is exposed to over five thousand ads daily.[22]

From a Buddhist perspective, consumerism is a false promise, as well as a recipe for ecological disaster. Buddhism teaches that happiness comes not from satisfying cravings but from ceasing to crave, from achieving an enlightened detachment from the misguided longings of the self. This approach yields both spiritual and environmental benefits, in the form of true inner peace and a smaller environmental footprint.

To be human, particularly in a consumerist society, is to be accosted by cravings. Mindful restraint, not indulgence, is the royal road to a sane and sustainable future.

Ordaining Trees

Stephanie Kaza writes about "green mentors," various parts of the natural world—trees, animals, rivers—which, when meditated upon, yield important wisdom and insight about the nature of reality. Other Buddhist writers have suggested that "the Buddha-nature"—the essence of the Buddha—can be found in all things, not just in human beings. In the 1990s, a group of Buddhist monks in Thailand showed what this teaching's implications were in real life. Let's hear their story as we wrap up our overview of Buddhist environmental teachings.

At the start of the twentieth century, over 75 percent of Thailand was covered by forests. By the late 1990s, as a result of extensive development efforts, less than 20 percent of the country remained forested. A number of Thai monks grew deeply concerned about the negative effect that this extensive logging, some of it state-sponsored and some of it illegal, had on many rural communities. One monk, Phrakhru Pitak, served in a remote village in northern Thailand in the 1970s. He watched deforestation lead to topsoil erosion, flood damage, and local people losing access to the forests that had, for many years, sustained them and their families. His district became among the poorest and driest in the country.[23]

Pitak and his fellow monks believed that Buddhism should be a vehicle to demonstrate compassion, reduce suffering, and to honor the interdependence of life. Tirelessly, he taught and preached about the Buddhist responsibility to respect the environment, to little effect. Susan Darlington, an ethnographer, wrote that if the villagers who heard him teach "saw a connection between their actions, their increasing poverty, and the environmental crisis, they did nothing about it."[24]

Finally, in 1990, Pitak took a bold step. He walked into the forest near his home village. He wrapped saffron orange robes around the trunk of a tree, the ritual act that signifies the ordination of a Buddhist monk.

This wasn't the first time that a Buddhist monk had ordained a tree—these ordinations had taken place sporadically over a fifteen-year period. But Pitak, along with a growing number of Buddhist monks, have increasingly used these tree ordinations as a powerful, symbolic expression of their religiously based education and conservation efforts.

Scholars believe that these tree ordinations, which the monks are careful to differentiate from the ordination of people, have made an impact. By using a symbolically powerful ritual act in a new way, these monks evoke deep, beyond-rational feelings in support of the environment. Because of the moral and emotional significance of the orange robes, these ordinations signify that Buddhists earn good *karma* by protecting the forest, and bad *karma* by destroying it. They teach that environmental stewardship is an act of compassion and reduces suffering. They remind villagers, business leaders, and government officials that Buddhism teaches respect for life. And by doing so, they help redefine the meaning and role of Buddhism in Thai society, for the good of the future of the country, its people, and the earth.

Summary of Key Themes

Buddhism teaches that meditation and mindfulness lead to a recognition of life's interconnectedness, which in turn evokes compassion toward all beings, including nature. In response to consumerist society that promotes the spiritually and environmentally dangerous illusion that we gain fulfillment via consumption, Buddhism teaches that we find enlightenment by detaching from our desires, by acting with compassion toward all life.

Two Different Peas in a Pod—Taoism, Confucianism, and Chinese Environmental Teachings

Home to over a billion people and to the fastest-growing environmental footprint on the planet, China has two religious traditions, Taoism and Confucianism, which have exerted the greatest influence on its culture. These two traditions, strikingly distinct in many ways, share several central themes. We'll review these first before exploring some of their distinctive teachings.

Élan Vital, Chinese Style

From the perspective of both Taoism and Confucianism, the universe is animated by a vital energy called *ch'i*. Many of the traditional Chinese practices designed to promote spirituality and health are organized to align our bodies and our surroundings, with the flow of *ch'i*. From the martial arts to *feng shui* (the practice of aligning our surroundings to maximize the flow of *ch'i*) to many traditional Chinese medical practices, ensuring the flow of *ch'i* is believed to represent the best way to sustain physical, spiritual, and moral well-being. And because *ch'i* is the essence of everything, it establishes an underlying connection and commonality between people and the natural world, not unlike the concept of *Brahman* within Hinduism. People and nature are, at their essence, literally interrelated.

World without End—or Beginning

Animated by *ch'i*, Chinese thinking sees the universe as having been spontane-ously self-generating—forever. No beginning. No end. Chinese religions lack a cre-ation story, instead seeing the universe as an "ongoing heartbeat of expansion (*yang*) and contraction (*yin*)."[25] Indeed, these traditions lack the sense that "creation" ever took place, in part because this would require the existence of an external creator, outside of the universe. From a Chinese perspective, the universe is a "web without a weaver," a reality in which nothing lies outside of an interconnected chain of exis-tence. This beginningless, endless state confounds most Western conceptions of real-ity, grounded as they are in a clear sense that "in the beginning," God created. Western traditions base their belief in nature's value on the belief that it is created and valued by God. Take away that foundation and Western eco-theologies become uncertain.

Interestingly, this lack of an external creator does not stop Chinese religion from believing in the existence of heaven or in the value of the environment. Heaven is simply part of a holistic universe, just like nature and people. And Chinese religions don't lack for resources that can make for a strong ethic of care for the environment. They simply don't base their beliefs on divine ownership of the earth, as we'll see now.

Three-Part Harmony

The concept of harmony and balance in the midst of change plays an important role in both Taoism and Confucianism. Mary Evelyn Tucker, a leading scholar of Chinese religion and the environment, refers to the "anthropocosmic" vantage point of Chinese religion, which sees heaven, nature, and people as part of a harmonious, three-part whole. Taoism and Confucianism see balance and harmony written into the very fabric of the earth, with opposing forces such as summer and winter, night and day, life and death as examples of a dynamic equilibrium that is an integral part of the world. These two traditions see the maintenance of balance and harmony on earth and in human life, and restoring this balance and harmony when it is lost, as a moral and spiritual priority.

Chinese landscape painting, an art form familiar to many, provides an excel-lent example of this harmony, the belief that the whole earth manifests a symphonic unity. These beautiful paintings, often large, depict a range of natural features, with a lovely balance of mountains and rivers, clouds and fields common to many of them. The natural world in Chinese painting, writes scholar Tu Wei-Ming, is multifaceted yet well-balanced "*ch'i* on display." In the midst of its majestic peaks, high waterfalls, deep valleys, and cultivated fields, nature's overall state is harmonious. For all their activity and broad scope, these paintings evoke peace.

People are present in most Chinese landscape paintings, but their role is modest. They fit into the landscape rather than dominating it, and their activities represent a small part of a much larger order. Some have observed that if the lens of European painting was, for centuries, focused on portraits and on human activity, its Chinese counterpart had a more wide-angle style. People were not the focus; there is no such thing as traditional Chinese portraiture. Rather, people are part of a broader reality.

Clearly, this "wide-angle" perspective offers a great asset for an environmentally friendly world. If we teach ourselves to see reality not as organized around us (anthropocentric) but as centered in the earth and in the universe (anthropocosmic—see above), perhaps we will learn to prioritize nature's needs, nature's well-being, alongside our own in our planning and decision making.

Taoism—Transformation Central

> *All streams flow to the sea because it is lower than they are.*
> *Humility gives it its power.*
>
> —*Tao Te Ching*, chapter 66

Taoism is a mystical, meditative tradition that emerged in approximately 500 BCE, and which sought to teach its followers to find the "Way,"—*Tao*. Taoism does not view nature in utilitarian terms. It teaches that human beings become able to find harmony, integrity, and alignment with *ch'i* by seeking naturalness and spontaneity, by eliminating the false structures of culture from the mind. Human beings grow in wisdom by seeking harmony with natural processes, not manipulating them. *Wu wei*, which is translated literally as "non-doing" or "effortless action," is central to Taoism.

Nature, which expresses itself perfectly and without premeditation or effort, is one of *wu wei's* best teachers. The *Tao Te Ching*, Taoism's preeminent text, teaches about *wu wei's* strength by pointing to natural processes and their paradoxical "soft power."

> *"Water is fluid, soft, and yielding. But water will wear away rock, which is rigid and cannot yield."*

and

> *"Nature does not hurry, yet everything is accomplished."*

and

> *"Do you have the patience to wait until your mud settles and the water is clear?"*

In an encomium to nature as the entity that points most clearly to the Tao, the *Tao Te Ching* states

Who understands Nature's way becomes all-cherishing;
Being all-cherishing he becomes impartial;
Being impartial he becomes magnanimous;
Being magnanimous he becomes part of Nature;
Being part of Nature he becomes one with Tao;
Being one with Tao he becomes immortal:
Though his body will decay, Tao will not.[26]

Like Buddhism, which it influenced significantly, Taoism features meditation as its primary method for achieving spiritual awareness. Meditation undoes the accretions and blockages that human culture has set in the way of spontaneity. Within a meditation practice, nature is a rich source of images that help remove these blockages.

The Taoist ideal is a largely monastic one of a life removed from politics or active social engagement. In such a life, meditation, simplicity, and closeness to nature create a Tao-like spontaneity within individuals and in human relations. Despite this somewhat narrow means of implementation, there are few traditions that hold a more positive view than Taoism of nature's energy, harmony, and ultimate value.

Confucianism's Social Ecology

If Taoism embodies a deep appreciation of nature in its unrefined form, Confucianism stresses the importance of virtuous leaders who have absorbed ancestral wisdom to maintain harmony between people and nature. Taoism looks to wilderness for wisdom. Confucianism seeks it in the *savoir faire* of *chun tzu*, wise persons who understand traditional teachings and who shape society to guide people toward moral, spiritual, and cultural maturity in relation to one another and the earth.

Tucker and others have written that Confucianism places a high value on "indebtedness to past generations and obligations to descendants." This is the meaning of "filial piety," a familiar Confucian phrase that describes the loyalty and respect that generations owe to one another. She writes that "within this moral framework there is the potential for evoking a sense of self-restraint and communal responsibility" that is needed for an environmentally sustainable society.[27] This is a familiar theme across many religions. Christian environmental leaders have spoken about the importance of passing a healthy environment to generations yet unborn. Jewish environmental leaders have used a similar thought pattern, using the teaching of *l'dor v'dor* (Hebrew for "generation to generation") to emphasize our debt to those who come after us. Creatively, Tucker expands the normal meaning of respect for elders within Confucianism to include nature, writing, "loyalty to elders, teachers, and those who have gone before may be broadened to include respect for the complex ecosystems and forms of life that have preceded humans."[28]

As previously implied, Confucianism focuses in significant part on the cultivation of wise leaders. Part of the mark of such a wise leader is that he or she understands nature as critical for sustaining human life and knows how to manage and oversee human engagement with nature in a way that promotes the well-being of each. If Taoism promotes enlightenment through close contact with nature, Confucianism teaches that wise leaders must ensure mutually beneficial relations between people and nature and that these are a *sine qua non* for society's survival.

Summary of Key Themes

Taoism and Confucianism see the world as constituted and animated by *ch'i,* a vital energy that is the essence of everything. Though these traditions do not teach that the world has a creator or beginning, they do assert that maintaining harmony between people and nature, through various spiritual practices and cultural traditions, represents an expression of ancient Chinese values. Taoism focuses on nature's power to transform our minds and to bring us into harmony with *ch'i,* while Confucianism focuses on cultivating mature leaders whose wise application of traditional teachings can maintain right relations between people, nature, and heaven.

One God, One World–Islamic Teachings on the Environment

"The earth has been created for me as a mosque and as a means of purification."

—Prophet Muhammad, *Al-Bukhari* I:331

Born in 570 CE in the city of Mecca, in modern-day Saudi Arabia, a boy named Abū al-Qāsim Muḥammad ibn ʾAbd Allāh ibn ʾAbd al-Muṭṭalib ibn Hāshim was orphaned at an early age. Raised by his beloved Uncle Abu Talib, he developed the habit by early adulthood of going on retreat to pray outside of his home city on the side of a mountain, at the back of a cave, in solitude. There, he calmed his mind and communed with the Ultimate One.

At the age of forty, in 610, this man—known as Muhammad—was in prayer in the mountainside cave. The Angel Gabriel appeared to him, and commanded him to "Recite!"[29] When he replied that he was unable to recite, the angel took hold of him in a ferocious embrace, three times. Finally, Muhammad submitted to divine authority. He recited. The revelation of the Qur'an, the sacred book of Islam, had begun.

And once again, a revelation vital to human spirituality, ethics, and religion had been given outdoors.

The world's 1.6 billion Muslims, spread across the globe but concentrated in Africa and Asia, are an emerging global force. They play a critical role in the future of the environment. Like its Abrahamic cousins Judaism and Christianity, Islam understands God as the universe's creator. In exploring our last of the major religions, we'll now look at several distinctly Islamic environmental teachings.

Unified

Part of the first "pillar of Islam"[30] is the teaching of the oneness of Allah (*Allah* is simply Arabic for God), a teaching with clear environmental connotations. Islam teaches that one way in which Allah's oneness is shown is in the unity of creation, its multifaceted harmony and efficacy. The sun and the moon are said to follow paths established by Allah, paths that enable them to serve their divine purpose. All parts of the natural world play their appointed role in promoting creation's functionality. And, in a manner similar to Bible's psalms, the Qur'an describes all of the universe joined in a collective praise of Allah—"Have you not regarded that to Allah prostrates whoever is in the heavens and whoever is on the earth, and the sun, the moon, and the stars, the mountains, the trees, and the animals and many of mankind?"[31]

Allah's oneness, a core Islamic teaching, is not an abstract fact. It is a living truth expressed majestically and beautifully in the complex, enlivened oneness of creation, a creation that bows collectively to worship its Maker.

Nature: "I Am Somebody"

Allah created every animal from water. Among them are some that creep upon their bellies, and among them are some that walk on two feet, and among them are some that walk on four. Allah creates whatever He wishes. Indeed Allah has power over all things. (Qur'an 24:45)[32]

There is no animal on the land, nor a bird that flies with its wings, but they are communities like yourselves. (Qur'an 6:38)[33]

I was a Hidden Treasure and I wanted to be known, so I created creatures in order to be known by them. (Hadith, transmitted by Ibn Arabî)[34]

Allah's unified creation, from the Qur'an's perspective, emerges from a common origin—water. But the bond, the commonality between the various members of the community of creation, is stronger than the physical element alone. The second quote above describes animals and birds as "communities." The Arabic word here—*ummah*—is significant. Normally used to describe human societies, the Qur'an uses *ummah* when referring to groups of peoples subject to Allah's "divine plan of salvation."[35] The term implies personhood and identity, individually and collectively.

It's striking, then, that animals and birds are referred to in this way. Here again, a sacred text establishes the concept of a community of creation, a community bound together not only by its common, divine origin or essence but also by its having identity, being a "somebody." Nature is not dumbly inert. It is alive. Responsive. And, as the third quotation above suggests, able to know God.

A Sign

> Among His signs is the creation of the heavens and the earth and whatever creatures He has scattered in them.
>
> —Qur'an 42:29[36]

The Arabic word *ayah* means "sign," "evidence," "revelation." It's a word regularly used to denote the existence of Allah as revealed by the Qur'an. Muslims consider each of the Qur'an's 6,236 verses to be an *ayah*, a sign pointing directly to God.

But there's a second meaning to this word. The world around us, the creation, is also an *ayah*. As Ibrahim Abdul Matin, an Islamic environmental writer, has said, "When we stand on a mountaintop, or at the edge of a great sea, or watch a glorious sunrise, we are immersed in the amazement of the signs Allah has spread out before us.... Our awe is a sense that we are part of the amazing beauty of those signs."[37]

In our overview of diverse religions, we've repeatedly encountered the belief that the natural world leads us toward and into the spiritual world.[38] Islam represents a powerful voice in this chorus, affirming nature's profound significance as a source of divine revelation.

Arabic for "Steward"

Islamic tradition holds that when the earth was created, Allah sought to identify who should be responsible for its care, who should serve as Allah's vicegerent, appointed by and accountable to Allah for creation's well-being. Allah first asked "the heavens and the earth and the mountains"[39] and other members of the wider community of creation to accept this responsibility. They declined, noting the difficulty of the task. The Qur'an says, "They were apprehensive of it."[40]

Human beings accepted this role, and were appointed as *Khalifa*, stewards of the planet, answerable to Allah at the Day of Judgment for the condition of the planet. Bluntly, with both pathos and humor, the Qur'an wonders whether people are up to the task, saying, "Indeed, he [man] is the most unfair and senseless."[41]

The role of vicegerent, of *Khalifa*, carries responsibility. Defined literally, the term means "an administrative deputy of a king or magistrate." In other words, a vicegerent is like God's business manager, a powerful role overseen by an even more powerful authority. Because of its importance, the people who occupy that role—all of us—are subject to God's judgment, a judgment that is ultimately focused on how we manage our own desires. Islam recognizes, as do all of the world's great religions, that people tend to indulge their own appetites and desires to excess, beyond their needs. A growing number of Muslim eco-theologians understand the environmental crisis to be the result of unchecked desires, both individually and collectively. Consequently, the Qur'an places a high value on the virtue of restraint, warning against those who have "taken [their] desire to be [their] god,"[42] reminding Muslims, "eat and drink, but do not waste; indeed He [*Allah*] does not like the wasteful."[43]

Trust and Verify

In assigning humanity the role of *Khalifa*, Allah directs humanity to fulfill the obligations of this office, to uphold the trust placed in us. The Arabic term that refers to this duty to fulfill our responsibilities, to fulfill God's trust, is *amana*. For Muslims, it is a serious word. It's a word that recognizes the magnitude of the expectations placed on us in our privileged role as *khalifa*. It's not a designation to be taken lightly. As Ibrahim Abdul Matin says: "God has given us the ability to make decisions over the land and the animals, and He trusts us to be responsible with this gift.... Our trust from God is not a license to pillage and destroy or to take from others—be they animals, plants, the ground, or the sky—without a just return. Our mandate from God dictates that we must praise the Creator, take care of the planet, and take care of one another."[44]

Balancing Act

The All-beneficent... created man [and] taught him articulate speech.
The sun and the moon are [disposed] calculatedly, and the herb and the
tree prostrate [to Allah]. He raised the sky and set up the balance.

—Qur'an 55:1-7[45]

There's a further dimension to our role as *khalifa*. Inherent in Allah's Creation, and central to a just society, is the concept of balance (Arabic: *mizan*), a divinely designed order that is represented in the earth's well-being. Islamic environmental leader Fazlun Khalid nicely captures the importance of this balance: "All creation has an order and a purpose and is in a state of dynamic balance. If the sun, the moon, the stars did not bow themselves, i.e., serve the purpose of their design, it would be impossible for life to function on earth. This is another way of saying that the natural order works because it is in submission to the Creator. It is Muslim in the original, primordial sense."[46]

Similar to the Chinese emphasis on the importance of maintaining harmony between people and planet, maintaining a similar balance is part of humanity's role. Through our behavior, we determine whether this balance is kept. We have the capacity to maintain it; we have the ability to disrupt it. And we are accountable for the choice we make.

Wudu with the Earth

Five times each day, observant Muslims take time to pray. But before they recite the obligatory prayers, Muslims ritually cleanse and purify themselves, a practice referred to as *wudu*. This practice involves the cleaning of one's face, hands, and feet. It is a central part of the ritual of Islamic prayer.

Normally, Muslims use water when they carry out these ablutions. But the Qur'an allows for the use of earth, soil, "dirt," if water is not available. Yes, you read correctly. The Qur'an teaches that we can be made spiritually clean by "washing" ourselves with dirt.

I've had the privilege of seeing this "dry *wudu*" carried out on several occasions. It is memorable. To watch a grown adult take modest handfuls of soil and to rub those, as if washing, on the front and back of their hands, on their feet, and on their face—the same parts of our body from which we most often wash to remove dirt—is a sight that shocks, confuses, and enlightens.

In a counterintuitive way, the practice of dry *wudu* represents a fitting way to close our exploration of Islamic teachings on the earth. Created by Allah, the earth retains an inherent goodness, a purity whose source is God. The earth not only sustains us with air, water, and food; it serves as a sign of Allah, and has the power to reconnect us to the source of our very being. That's what dry *wudu* signifies—the ever-fresh, ever-pure, ever-living presence of the divine.

Even if it seems to make us dirty.

Summary of Key Themes

Islam teaches that Allah, the universe's creator, has given humanity the challenging responsibility of being *kahlifa*, stewards of the earth. This responsibility, which includes our duty to maintain nature's balance and to respect its status as a sign that points toward Allah, is a serious task for which we are held accountable. The natural world is not a collection of inanimate "things" that we can use in any way that we want. Rather, it is a community, a gathering of *ummah* that have their own identity and status in the eyes of God.

By exercising self-restraint and by reminding ourselves of the high value that Allah places on the earth, we are to discharge our responsibilities as its caretaker with dignity and skill.

Many Faiths, Shared Beliefs

So at the end of this survey, what are we to make of this collection of religious teachings on the environment? Are there common themes that emerge from these diverse traditions? The answer is yes. Three primary themes can be found in all of these traditions' teachings on the environment: spirituality, stewardship, and justice.

Spirituality

Each of the religions we've explored recognizes the beauty, majesty, intricacy, diversity, and power of nature as a source of spiritual inspiration, as a point of profound connection with the divine. Whether as a sign of the Creator's majesty in the Abrahamic traditions or an expression of ultimate harmony in the Eastern traditions, the trend is clear. The natural world reveals the world of the sacred.

Part of the spirituality that nature supports is a sense that we belong to a wider, interconnected, beyond-human community. For the Abrahamic faiths, this interconnectedness is often expressed in worshipful terms—with all earth's creatures and natural features gathered in a collective praise of the Creator. In the Dharmic tradition, the idea of a shared essence—whether *Brahman* or Buddha-nature—establishes this common bond. In the Chinese world, the interconnection is felt most strongly in the bonds between people, planet, and past and future generations. Regardless, the essential interconnectedness of heaven and earth is a fundamental religious teaching. Whether through a sense of kinship or shared origin or common essence, or through the sense that the entire planet is gathered in a collective, primal form of devotion, the world's religions teach that our lives are intertwined with the planet and with the world of the spirit.

Stewardship

Amidst their diversity, the world's traditions teach that our job is to care not only for our family and friends, or for our fellow human beings, but also for the planet. The Abrahamic traditions use the stewardship model most commonly, in which the earth is created by and belongs to God, and is cared for by people. The Eastern traditions—both Dharmic and Chinese—place a high value on the transformation and enlightenment of the individual into a mature, self-restrained, ecologically responsible member of society. All of these traditions, in their own ways, assert that there is a very real sense in which the earth is not our property. We may use it to satisfy our needs, as a source of sustenance and joy. But ultimately it is not our own. We must learn to keep our desires in check, restrain ourselves, if the we and the earth are to have a future.

There are many real differences between the world's religions. But none of them teaches that life's purpose or true meaning comes from consuming as much as we can. We are called to watch over the earth. To protect. To guard. To maintain. To preserve. Not to destroy.

Justice

Implicit in all the religions we've examined is a sense of rightness, or justice, in relation to the earth. Indigenous traditions teach clearly that we must treat the natural world not only with decency, but with the respect due to an elder, a member of our family. Buddhism and Hinduism speak of the compassion we owe to all other beings, as well as to each other. The Abrahamic traditions speak directly of social justice, focusing particularly on those people who are most vulnerable, least powerful. An emerging theme in Judaism, Christianity, and Islam is the justice due to the most vulnerable people who suffer disproportionately from pollution. All traditions are coming to a deeper understanding of the just claims that future generations have on us, and on our treatment of the Earth.

Whether between powerful and vulnerable human beings, between people and nature, or between present and future generations, we must recognize that our understanding of fairness and rightness, of decency and justice, must be expanded to include the earth. Otherwise, we will have no justice at all.

Discussion Questions

1. Think of your own religious tradition, and then think over the other traditions explored in this book. What are the most interesting or attractive teachings from traditions outside of your own? Why? Which teachings are least appealing to you? Why?

2. Often, we recognize new dimensions of our own traditions when we study the traditions of others. Has this chapter, or this book, given you insights into your own tradition? If so, what are these insights?

Part 2
The Earth Itself

Chapter 5

What's in a Word?

The Many Meanings of *Environment*

Where We've Been and Where We're Headed

We're now entering a different stage of our journey in relation to faith and the environment. So far, we've examined the spiritual experiences that people have outdoors, the deep, powerful connections with God and the Spirit that take place in nature. We've then looked at teachings from the Bible, and from other great religions, in relation to the earth. Our focus has been on the best of our relationship with the natural world, on the ways in which it inspires and moves us deeply, and on the wisdom from sacred writings that suggest how we ought to view, respect, and treasure it.

Soon, we'll turn toward an actual overview of the condition of nature itself, an overview of the world's major natural systems, the systems that support and represent the very fabric of life. In the chapter following this one, we're going to look at how these systems are doing—where they stand, and what humanity has to do with that. We'll focus on the air, water, and land that sustains us, and the plants and animals with whom we share the planet and on whom we depend for food and companionship.

A Narrative Hinge

This chapter represents an interlude, a hinge between these two parts of the book. It is not focused on biblical or moral or religious teachings. Nor is it focused on scientific evidence, factual data. It is, instead, focused on our perceptions of nature, the common stories, narratives, through which our culture views the word *environment*.

Counter to the old marketing saying, perception may not be reality. But perception does represent our understanding of reality. Subsequently, it influences our behavior profoundly. If one considers the topic of the environment, one will see that there are several common reactions that this topic evokes within our culture. It's the hypothesis of this chapter that these reactions, these perceptions, matter a lot. Here's why.

These perceptions provide the emotional and cognitive frameworks out of which our behavior toward the natural world arises. These perceptions largely determine the policies that our society's institutions use to determine and justify their treatment of the environment—our governments and corporations, our educational, cultural, and religious institutions. More than our outdoor spiritual experiences and theological, moral teachings on the one hand and the earth's actual physical state of well-being or distress on the other hand, these common perceptions are our society's functional definitions of the topic "environment." These perceptions or narratives have a greater influence on our behavior toward the environment than do any other combination of factors. They carry greater influence than the facts or the values we believe we hold.

In the best of worlds, these narratives should provide a bridge that mediates between human needs, the conditions needed for a healthy planet, the wisdom of science, and our deepest human values, enabling us to create and maintain abundant life on a thriving planet. But reality is trickier than that. The purpose of this chapter, then, is to look at the most widespread perceptions, the most common narratives that our culture employs in relation to the environment, and to assess them in relation to this overarching goal.

This chapter represents a pause, a temporary stopping point. It is an interlude when we stop and think about what the word *environment* means in our culture, and what the implications of those meanings are.

What's in a Word? Environmental Narratives

It doesn't take a genius to recognize that the word *environment* evokes feelings—strong ones. For some people, it evokes a sense of beauty and well-being and represents a high priority to which they are deeply committed. For others it signals a political and cultural agenda with which they disagree, even if they care about conserving nature. Still for others it serves as a reminder of regulations with which their businesses must comply. The word *environment*, then, means different things to different people.

There are several common ways in which people think about the environment, common lenses through which US media and political culture have viewed this topic and the meaning of this word. As noted above, I refer to these shared stories, these common perspectives, as "environmental narratives." Each of these narratives has a unique "personality," a standard set of concerns, emotions, and reactions to the word *environment* itself. Growing out of their personality, each narrative asserts a different claim on us, emotionally, intellectually, and behaviorally. If we're not aware of these environmental narratives and which of them we resonate with, it can become easy to lose sight of the actual environment itself because we become identified with the narratives themselves and blinded by their sway.

Testing the Spirits

Most people identify with more than one of these narratives, and many people find common ground with several of them. That's understandable—the goal is not to have one monolithic way to understand such a vital, massive topic. But for people of faith striving to discern God's will for creation and for our relationship to it, we need to understand these environmental narratives and be able to evaluate them, make decisions about their trustworthiness and deeper implications, their veracity and value. In the New Testament, the First Letter of John reads, "Dear friends, don't believe every spirit. Test the spirits to see if they are from God because many false prophets have gone into the world" (4:1). We should approach the topic of environmental narratives in the same way. We should understand what these narratives say, where they come from, and what they imply—because they are important. These narratives guide and influence our treatment of the very physical source and sustenance of our lives as well as our behavior toward one of God's greatest works—nature. Only by evaluating these narratives will we become mature in our ability to understand the challenges that the environment faces, and to respond properly.

Nature as Eden—The Paradise Narrative

The first narrative we'll discuss is the Paradise Narrative. From this perspective, nature is a stunningly beautiful, awe-inspiring, fragile place, which should be highly respected and carefully treated. Those who believe in this narrative often describe nature as benign and nonthreatening. They worry about nature's vulnerability to people, not about people's vulnerability to natural forces. Nature here represents a state of perfection that restores us, heals us from our overexposure to our polluted, degraded industrial and postindustrial world. As Henry David Thoreau wrote in Walden, one of the most revered writings of the environmental movement, "We need the tonic of wildness...We require that all things be mysterious and unexplorable, that land and sea be indefinitely wild, unsurveyed and unfathomed by us because unfathomable. We can never have enough of nature."[1]

There are several aspects of this narrative that should be noted. First, it prioritizes nature's beauty and appreciation of that beauty. And while the appreciation of nature's beauty and majesty are as old as human consciousness, this particular narrative reflects the lack of an appreciation that we must work the Earth in order to survive. In addition, the Paradise narrative treats nature as solely benign and lacks an appreciation that natural disasters, plagues, and various diseases are as "natural" as clean water and air. As such, it is a narrative that may appeal most strongly to those in the First World, to those in industrial and postindustrial societies, to the wealthier people on the planet who are relatively well-shielded from the power of nature to harm as well as to heal or who have the time to appreciate nature's beauty.

Second, the narrative focuses largely on nature's soothing, friendly qualities—its restorative, re-creational value. This narrative doesn't reflect an understanding that nature's "circle of life" is filled with violence as well as beauty, with predation as well as cooperation. Nor does this narrative account for our need to work the land, to use nature in order to live, or for the necessary tragedy involved in our relationship with the earth, an unavoidable taking of life, for example, every time we eat.

These observations aren't meant to discount the importance of the Paradise Narrative, merely to probe it more deeply. And as for the value of this narrative? The first chapter of this book, which explored the vital importance of outdoor spiritual experiences, speaks passionately to that. I don't intend this rejoinder to invalidate the value of those experiences but rather to probe our understanding of them more deeply.

Seriously—The Scientific Narrative

The second common environmental narrative is the Scientific Narrative. This narrative uses the language of physical observation, numbers, complexity, and fact to communicate about the earth. Its tone is serious and studied. It is often a narrative both of revelation and concern, as it relays remarkable insights not only about how the natural world works but also about the impact of human actions on the planet. And, especially early in the study of any given phenomenon, it involves probability rather than certainty, the balancing of possibility and the unknown.

Because of its complexity, the Scientific Narrative can be difficult to follow. Consider this representative passage from a report of the Intergovernmental Panel on Climate Change, the world's authoritative scientific body on that particular environmental issue: "The globally averaged combined land and ocean surface temperature data as calculated by a linear trend, show a warming of 0.85 [0.65 to 1.06] °C3, over the period 1880 to 2012, when multiple independently produced datasets exist. The total increase between the average of the 1850–1900 period and the 2003–2012 period is 0.78 [0.72 to 0.85] °C, based on the single longest dataset available."[2] This kind of language is admirably precise. But it is hard to follow for the scientifically uninitiated, and it doesn't quite capture the soul for most of us.

To be fair, there is another aspect to the scientific narrative—its ability to evoke awe through its observations and descriptions of the earth and the universe. What the Scientific Narrative lacks in emotion, it often makes up in the fascinating, minutely detailed images of physical reality that it offers up. For example, the recent Census of Marine Life, a decade-long exploration of the inhabitants of the oceans, yielded jaw-dropping reports of creatures of the deep ocean, images so otherworldly as to be unbelievable. One of these creatures, the angler fish, is a fantastically odd creature that lives in the pitch-black darkness of mile-deep ocean waters. It has a bone spur protruding forward from its forehead that juts out over its jaws. The spur has a bio-luminescent tip that glows in the murky darkness, attracting prey. For its size, the angler fish has an enormous mouth and gigantic, jagged, translucent teeth, enabling it to swallow prey almost twice its size. It is captivating, repulsive, menacing, and awe-inspiring at once.

Or consider the images from the Hubble telescope, which provides us with images from deep space in a way that no other human invention has ever done. With high-definition clarity, Hubble's images reveal intricate, smoky nebulae, galaxies with spiraling arms reaching into space's deep darkness, star clusters with, literally, millions of points of light—with each of these features millions of light years across and separated from us by unimaginable distances. These awe-evoking kinds of images, from the ocean's depths to the far cosmic reaches, are another facet of the Scientific Narrative. They represent a generous gift to us all.

One final observation about the Scientific Narrative. For many centuries, religion and the arts were the source of much of society's language of awe, the words and phrases and images that evoked astonishment and wonder. In recent centuries, scientific language has taken on much of that role. Through its descriptions of so many aspects of the natural world, from strange creatures to unthinkably powerful subatomic forces to mind-bending intergalactic distances, science now makes frequent, significant contributions to our collective language of amazement.

Apocalypse Now—The Environmentalist Narrative

Black, sooty smoke belching from industrial smokestacks. Discolored, fouled water streaming out of the end of a corroded metal pipe. Birds, in the wake of an oil spill with wings smothered in black ooze. These disturbing images bear the distinct, stylistic imprint of the Environmentalist Narrative.

This narrative holds that human activity is causing grave, irreparable harm to the environment. It seeks to sound the alarm, to rouse people to the fact that unthinkable harm is happening—that our mistreatment of the natural world, our home, is leading to its destruction and to ours. If the Scientific Narrative is emotionally reserved, the Environmentalist Narrative is emotionally supercharged. Read the websites of most environmental organizations and you'll feel the fear, anger, and dread quickly. There's an apocalyptic quality to this narrative, a sense that if we do not awaken and act, we are doomed.

At its best, the Environmentalist Narrative expresses a passionate concern for nature, a concern that's often absent from our society's consciousness and decision making about actions that impact the planet. This narrative represents an important call for attention, a warning about serious danger, and a frustration that we do not take more seriously the well-being of the earth. And within a short span of several decades, this narrative has helped create much positive change, including legislation and regulation that has reduced many forms of pollution. Personally, I am sympathetic to this narrative. I believe that many of its claims are on-target, many of its concerns well-founded.

However, many people find this narrative off-putting, feeling that it represents a left-leaning cultural and political worldview. They find its tone and tactics polarizing, antibusiness, and alarmist. Critics point to many environmentalists' deep-seated mistrust of genetically modified food or traditional opposition to fluoride in drinking water as evidence that this narrative promotes a shortsighted mistrust of humanity's technological ingenuity. Some critics go so far as to suggest that environmentalists harbor animosity toward human progress.

The jury remains out on many of these criticisms of this narrative. Alarmism is neither inherently on- or off-target, and the preponderance of scientific evidence appears to validate the importance of the Environmentalist Narrative. But it's important to acknowledge that in the present moment, this narrative's apocalyptic quality is both galvanizing and alienating and likely to remain so.

Damn the Torpedoes—The Skeptics Narrative

Bjorn Lomborg is the bane of many environmentalists. The author of *The Skeptical Environmentalist* and the subsequent *Cool It—The Skeptical Environmentalist's Guide to Global Warming*, Lomborg has received enormous attention for arguing that many environmentalist claims are "based on emotional rather than strictly scientific assumptions." Responding to the emotionality of the Environmentalist Narrative, he asserts that "panic is neither warranted nor a constructive place from which to deal with any of humanity's problems, not just global warming."[3] He goes on to suggest that instead of making dramatic changes to address issues such as climate change, we should take a more gradual approach, mindful that we have limited resources and that investments in the environment inevitably result in other areas, such as aid to the poor, being reduced.

Welcome to the Skeptic Narrative, in which the primary target is emotionally overheated environmentalists and the threat they pose to human well-being. Bjorn Lomborg is a "soft skeptic." His brand of skepticism doesn't doubt that climate change is happening or that humanity is causing it, unlike the cruder versions of the Skeptic Narrative that represent simplistic, reactive denial. However, he blunts fear about the climate crisis by lifting up the most conservative, best-case interpretations of the scientific findings and by expressing optimism about humanity's capacity to adapt in response to environmental changes.

Doubtless, the Skeptic Narrative, with its tendency to deny the severity of various environmental threats, reflects that timeless human tendency to play ostrich, sticking our heads in the sand in the face of uncomfortable truths. And at its best, the Skeptic Narrative can provide a moderating emotional influence in response to the intensity of the Environmentalist Narrative and a challenge to environmentalists to make their case using both "heat and light," emotion and reason. But at its worst, this narrative seeks to make us dangerously comfortable in the face of real dangers and to justify the status quo by denying or altering reality. Despite its popularity in some quarters, it's a problematic narrative, a seductive and reactive one that we might expect to find in the midst of environmentally troubled times.

Breaking the Bank? Or the Next Big Thing? The Economic Narrative

The photograph depicts an angry group of demonstrators, marching under a hot summer sun, carrying signs that say things such as "People are more important than fish."

The scene? A demonstration organized by farmers and farming communities in the Pacific Northwest, arguing that more water should be used to support farms and less water set aside to protect fish and the health of a river.

This scene represents a traditional view, an old form of the Economic Narrative on the environment. Its logic is simple. More environmental protection means less economic growth and vice versa. This old narrative is the heart of the argument that many people use to criticize environmental regulation as being a drag on the economy.

Another signboard, this time representing an intended joke, offers a variation on this theme. It's a sign that looks exactly like the green logo for the upscale, organic food chain *Whole Foods*. But if you look closely, this version of the sign doesn't say *Whole Foods*. Instead, it reads *Whole Paycheck*, implying that organic food, and by extension environmental protection, is a luxury good, something only the wealthy can afford.

But in the past decade, a new version of the Economic Narrative has emerged, organized under the banner of green jobs. Rather than rehashing the tired tirade that environmental protection carries an unsustainably high financial cost, this new narrative argues that businesses that create economic and environmental benefits are the wave of the future, that inevitably our economy must create financial and ecological well-being instead of pitting them against each other. Groups such as the Blue Green Alliance, a coalition of labor unions and environmental groups, represent an important, popular base of support for this narrative, and call for investments in "green infrastructure" that can create jobs at home while investing in industries such as water treatment, renewable energy manufacturing, and mass transit that will constitute the foundation of future prosperity.

There's no question that there can be an up-front cost for environmental protection, an initial financial investment that must be made. But leaders in the growing field of environmental entrepreneurship, such as the libertarian Property and Environmental Rights Council, have asserted with increasing influence that prosperity doesn't preclude clean air and water. And it's interesting to note that study after study has shown that there are very real economic benefits that follow from investments in various forms of pollution reduction. Take, for example, the history of the Clean Air Act, a major piece of US environmental legislation from the 1970s. Peer-reviewed research has shown repeatedly that this piece of legislation, in 2010 alone, reduced air pollution that prevented "160,000 premature deaths, 130,000 heart attacks, millions of cases of respiratory problems such as acute bronchitis and asthma attacks, and 86,000 hospital admissions. [In addition, this legislation] prevented thirteen million lost workdays, improving worker productivity which contributes to a stronger economy . . . [and] kept kids healthy and in school, avoiding 3.2 million lost school days due to respiratory illness and other diseases caused or exacerbated by air pollution." The summary of the research on the economic impacts of the Act noted that cleaner air improved crop and timber yields, and that by 2020 the Act will have created economic benefits outweighing its costs by a ratio of thirty to one.[4]

As these figures and the anecdotes above suggest, the emergent version of the Economic Narrative, which unites environmental protection with economic prosperity, is destined to grow in influence.

The Sound of Silence—The Absence Narrative

Several years ago, I spent a week at a retreat center in northern Vermont. It was an incredible experience. Solar power provided the energy that heated water for our showers. Biogas generated by the processing the waste of local farm animals was used for cooking fuel. Most of the food came from within a one-hundred-mile radius, supplied by small farms across the state. Many of the cooking implements, and all of the bowls and spoons that we used to eat our food, had been carved from trees felled on the farm itself. That week, one of our activities involved carving our own wooden spoon. I carved a small baby spoon for my daughter, who was to be born two months later.

While I was carving the spoon, I looked up at the tree from whose fallen branch the spoon was being carved. I realized at that moment that for most of human history, this was how people had lived—the stuff of their existence coming from natural resources that they themselves had touched, seen, lived with. Nature was, unavoidably, present. It was a vital source of the materials of everyday life, of the food on the dinner table, of the tools of various trades—of everything. There was little question about where things came from. Vegetables didn't come from supermarkets. They came from the ground, most often ground that was within a stone's throw.

In reviewing the most common environmental narratives that our culture has to offer, I've saved the most common one for last. It's the Absence Narrative. This is the default, lived narrative for most people, most of the time. Essentially, the Absence Narrative locates the environment at the intersection of "nonexistent" and "taken for granted." This narrative's underlying assumption is that we do not need to worry, think, or concern ourselves about the environment—the air, water, and soil that makes our lives possible. Supermarkets, big box stores, gas stations, and the Internet supply us with what we need in order to live. The environment barely registers.

This narrative, unthinkable for most of human history, has become our new normal within barely a century. Increasing technological sophistication, urbanization, and wealth have made it possible for the vast majority of people to move off the farm, a primary connection with nature for most of human history. As late as 1870, over 70 percent of the US population was employed in agriculture,[5] their livelihood tied with unavoidable directness to Mother Nature. By 2008, that figure had dropped to less than 2 percent,[6] and author Richard Louv had watched his book *Last Child in the Woods—Saving Our Children from Nature Deficit Disorder* become a best-seller. The book analyzed the many ways in which people have become disconnected from the natural world and called on educators, policy makers, and spiritual leaders to make sure that "no child was left inside."

Vanishing Act

To a meaningful degree, the lessening of our contact with nature reflects humanity's technological, economic, and cultural advancement, which has gone hand in hand with an increase in human lifespan and economic well-being in many parts of the world. There is much to be grateful for in these advancements. It is naïve and wrong to undervalue them. But an unintended consequence of the growth of our power has been the ways in which it makes nature vanish from our sight in regards to the production of the energy, food, clothing, and thousands of consumer goods that constitute the material dimension of our lives.

If out of sight has often meant out of mind, this creates problems in itself. We've discussed the spiritual impoverishment that a nature-deprived life entails, but there's more at stake than this. There's a broad lack of awareness of the negative health impacts of polluted air, soil, and water, diminished access to healthy food, and the other environmental health threats that shorten millions of lives around the world, health impacts that are not insignificant. Research from respected expert sources such as MIT shows, for instance, that air pollution is responsible for more than two hundred thousand premature US deaths annually.[7] Pollution, omnipresent, remains invisible to many, off our collective radar screens. And because we don't have the eyes to see it, we underestimate the threat it poses.

If nature's vanishing act at the hands of human advancement has been a mixed blessing for us, it has generally meant worse things for nature itself. We'll explore the harmful effects of human activity on the natural world in a later chapter. Suffice it to say that, for nature, invisibility has meant overuse and exploitation. It has placed us on a collision course with the planet's capacity to host us healthily.

When it comes to the environment, the Absence Narrative has not made our hearts grow fonder. The single most dominant environmental narrative in our culture, the Absence Narrative has hidden nature's absolutely necessary, life-giving qualities from plain sight, and has hidden our misuse of nature's bounty, God's bounty, from sight as well. It renders invisible both nature's beauty and its degradation. It blunts our appreciation for one of God's great gifts. Because it renders the earth largely invisible, it disables an important potential of our sense of sorrowful guilt for earth's disintegration and our own drive toward more respectful treatment for the planet. But despite the fact that this narrative clearly needs to go, it remains the default position for most of society most of the time. By making nature absent and invisible, the narrative itself becomes the elephant in the room, a perception (or, ironically, a lack of a perception) that forces everything else to work around it.

Evaluating the Narratives

Paradise. Science. Environmentalist. Skeptic. Economic. Absence. These are some of the most influential environmental narratives within society, some of the most common ways in which we perceive nature, our relationship to it, and our responsibility for it. I'll close by suggesting two criteria by which faith communities should evaluate the value and veracity of these and other environmental narratives, the kinds of questions we should ask ourselves when we consider these different ways of accounting for the value of the environment, and for our treatment of it.

Abundant Life

Two criteria should represent the core of a religious response to the environment and concerns related to it. The first criterion is that a genuinely religious environmental narrative should support the flourishing of life. It should result in beliefs and actions that support both abundance and quality of life, both human life and beyond-human. This criterion asserts a fundamental purpose to the natural world, the creation—which is to support our existence and the existence of the many other forms of life.

This first criterion is basic. It values existence. It asserts a purpose for the earth, and for its systems and processes. It holds that the creation, in all its dynamism and change, in all its struggles and manifestations, is ultimately on the side of being, and that this being is fundamental, valuable, worth protecting. It believes that the earth, and life, is good.

Instrument and Icon

The second criterion is that a religious environmental narrative must affirm both an instrumental and an intrinsic, iconic value to nature in a manner that supports the overall goal of the first criterion—supporting abundant life. This means that a religious narrative on the environment should affirm people's needs to work with and use natural resources, that we shouldn't fall prey to a sentimental sense that we can or should somehow live without impacting nature. We all need to eat and to consume in order to live—and over a billion people on the earth, who live on less than $2 per day in crippling poverty, need to consume much more than they already do.

But this rightful need to use nature to support our own well-being shouldn't be divorced either from an enlightened sense of self-interest (human life, for instance, does requires clean air and water) or from a basic respect for nature's intrinsic worth and for the idea that nature has value outside of its instrumental value to us. Nature is not just there for us. It is there for itself. Its simple existence gives God pleasure. On its own, it serves as a form of witness and worship, praise and devotion to the divine.

All of the religion that we reviewed affirmed that nature holds this combination of intrinsic and iconic value, that it serves human needs while retaining a basic dignity of its own. I won't pretend that managing the tension between these two poles is easy, or free of conflict. But it's only by maintaining this dynamic tension that we will arrive at a genuinely religious resolution to the environmental challenges that face us.

Discussion Questions

1. This chapter describes several environmental narratives—Paradise. Science. Environmentalist. Skeptic. Economic. Absence. With which of these narratives do you identify the most? The least? Why?

2. Are there other narratives that should be added to this list? What are they?

3. This chapter suggests that the two criteria by which people of faith should judge environmental narratives are: Do the narratives support abundance of life? And, does the narrative support both an instrumental and intrinsic value to nature? What is your reaction to these two criteria? What criteria would be most important for you?

Chapter 6

The Pale Blue Dot

Our Remarkable Planet

In 1990, the Voyager 1 spacecraft was 3.7 billion miles from Earth, preparing to leave the solar system. The eminent astronomer Carl Sagan asked NASA to turn its camera, one last time, back toward Earth for a photograph. The subsequent image, which came to be called Pale Blue Dot, showed a miniscule blue pixel suspended in the vastness of space. "From this distant vantage point," Sagan wrote in his 1994 book *The Pale Blue Dot,*

> The Earth might not seem of any particular interest. But for us, it's different. Look again at that dot. That's here. That's home. That's us. On it everyone you love, everyone you know, everyone you ever heard of, every human being who ever was, lived out their lives....The Earth is a very small stage in a vast cosmic arena....[But] the Earth is the only world known, so far, to harbor life....To me, [this image] underscores our responsibility to deal more kindly with one another and to preserve and cherish the pale blue dot, the only home we've ever known.[1]

Prepare to be amazed.

And prepare to think.

It's time for a tour of the earth, a time to appreciate the remarkable splendor and complexity of nature, to appreciate the foundation for our life that nature represents. It's also time to look, with the truthfulness that is fitting for faith communities, at the impact that we're having on the planet.

Here are five introductory observations before we begin this tour, five guideposts to help shepherd us through this high-speed journey.

Between the Earth and a Hard Place

First, there is an underlying narrative here, an overarching theme to this chapter. I believe that it is an honest, accurate narrative and that each of its parts must be taken seriously. Here it is:

The natural world is a remarkable gift that sustains an abundance of life.

Humanity is currently treating the earth in a way that is diminishing its life-supporting, life-giving power, often dramatically.

If we change our ways, the earth can be restored, healed, renewed. It can regain its God-given, life-supporting purpose. We can be agents of God's love for creation.

If we do not change, the earth will increasingly lose its wondrous capacity to support life. Hundreds of millions of people, along with millions of other forms of life, will suffer. Many will die. We will degrade one of God's greatest works.

Currently, we have not changed our ways in a manner approaching what's needed to support abundant life. We have begun to awaken to the challenge, the crisis that faces us. But our repentance is, so far, incomplete.

We must choose.

At the start of this scientifically oriented chapter, this is an openly moral, religious narrative. It represents a vital context within which to understand the findings of science.

Hold Fast to Amazement and Hope

Second, in the face of this challenging narrative, it can be easy to feel overwhelmed, to the point of despair. And while the challenges we face are great and feelings of disorientation and sadness are understandable and important, they must not, ultimately, give way to despair or helplessness.

We have a lot of work to do. We need to arouse our energies, our passion, our gifts, and strengths to restore the earth. It can be done. But to summon these vital energies, to meet these challenges, we need to believe that change can happen. That we can make progress. That we are able, working together and with God's help, to succeed. Ecosystems consistently demonstrate a remarkable ability to recover and to thrive, given a chance. The cause is not lost.

But, as we'll see, we face a daunting, very real collection of challenges of "wicked problems" that have multiple causes and no easy solutions. But humanity has faced down wicked problems in the past and can rise to the occasion again. There's an Irish saying of which I'm fond: "Is this a private fight, or can anyone join in?" This represents the energized attitude that's required.

Holding doggedly, stubbornly fast to the gift of amazement that the earth gives to us is one valuable way to remain spiritually enabled to respond to the environmental crisis. Remaining amazed reminds us what we're fighting for. It reminds us why we care. It lifts up our spirits. It empowers us to hope. Throughout this chapter, I'll offer examples of nature's remarkable qualities or attributes, often using reference to size, numbers, or extraordinary characteristics as a shorthand means of signaling amazement. The purpose of these examples is not voyeurism, but rather an insistence that we not become dulled to the miracle of creation. Years ago, Rabbi Abraham Joshua Heschel, one of the great religious leaders of the twentieth century, wrote, "Our goal should be to live life in radical amazement...to get up in the morning and look at the world in a way that takes nothing for granted. Everything is phenomenal; everything is incredible; never treat life casually. To be spiritual is to be amazed."[2] That is the attitude we require in order to protect the earth.

Ironically, in the face of grave challenges that we learn of from the scientific community, it is a spiritual sensibility that empowers us to respond. We must remain amazed—at the remarkable beauty and goodness of creation, and at the remarkable majesty and love of its Creator. We must keep hope alive.

Immune to Spin

Third, we must recognize that the earth itself, and the effects of the condition of the earth, are immune to human "spin." Nothing that we *say* affects the condition of the earth. It's what we *do* to the earth that matters. Our environmental actions carry inevitable consequences, consequences that cannot be explained away. We cannot talk our way out of environmental problems that we have acted ourselves into. The late Senator Daniel Patrick Moynihan is said to have remarked, "You are entitled to your own opinion, but you are not entitled to your own facts." This speaks directly to our current situation. A commitment to truth is a vital dimension to being a religious person concerned about the environment.

As in every area of life, the truth can be hard. It can challenge our preconceptions, our comfort, our sense of who we are. But a commitment to truthfulness is a precondition to a religious engagement of the environment.

What we say will not change the reality of pollution. Nor will it alter the impact that pollution has on people and on the environment. Nature, in this way, has an inviolable commitment to the truth. It is, thank God, immune to our spin. It is inalienably honest.

We need to be likewise.

Care about the Poor

Religious communities have a particular lens through which they view many social concerns. In all areas of life, faith communities care about the impact of society's actions on the poor, the most vulnerable. This must hold true when it comes to the environment.

As we'll see, it's the poor who consistently suffer pollution's worst impacts, locally and globally. Faith communities must raise our awareness about this. We must allow ourselves to feel the same level of sadness when we hear about those suffering from air pollution or toxic exposures as we do when we hear about people who lack food or shelter. We must find ways to evoke within our communities a deep reservoir of concern for those whose health suffers from dirty air and contaminated soil. We must learn to express compassion, an ancient religious virtue, for those whose suffering is caused by a degraded planet.

The Wider Community of Life

Finally, faith communities must learn to recognize that we are part of a larger community of life, and that we have bonds of care and responsibility with the natural world. We must develop new ways of feeling this sense of kinship with nature. We must accept that the rest of creation deserves a greater degree of "standing" when it comes to our behavior, that we must take nature into account when making our decisions, individually and collectively.

The idea that nature has standing and is an actual character in our lives runs counter to consumerist sensibilities, which view the earth as a simple storehouse of resources at our disposal, an inert warehouse of supplies that has no claim on us. And because of the spread of consumerism and our disconnectedness from the earth (see the Absence Narrative in the previous chapter), we have no common vocabulary to use to describe our bond for the earth in "mainstream" terms. Sadly, we aren't good at expressing our bonds, emotional or moral, with the rest of the natural world. Ironically, for many people, talking about our bonds with nature feels unnatural.

Faith communities can be places where we find this new vocabulary of respect and care, of compassion and love, for the natural world. It will take time for this language to emerge, and for these new bonds to become conscious. But it's vital to get this process started. While the earth may not be affected, directly, by the language and frameworks that we use, our own behavior is. We need, and the earth needs, language that supports an ethically and emotionally healthy bond with nature.

Around the World

It's now time for an abbreviated global tour, a look at some of the basics of the nature of nature—the water, land, and air that constitute and binds our lives. These brief descriptions, which are only the most incomplete of introductions, represent an effort to empower people of faith to think more holistically about the natural world, to understand the stunning scope of creation, the challenging threats it faces, and the outlines of what we must do in order to protect nature and ourselves. Too often, religious leaders and faith communities steer away from environmental concerns because they don't understand the basic science behind the issues or the fundamentals of an understanding of earth's systems. This needs to change.

While these next several sections are far too short to accomplish that, I hope they point in that direction and offer an introduction to a way of thinking that religious groups need to embrace in order to develop a new commitment to life on Earth.

Water

Life first appeared in water. We start our journey there.

Most people think of water as relatively stationary, located in a specific place such as a river, lake, or ocean. They're wrong.

Water, always, is on the move. It's constantly changing states, from liquid to vapor to precipitation to ice, over and over again, blown by the wind and carried by currents across the globe. Water can shape-shift in the blink of an eye at the instant of evaporation, and over the millennia as a glacier is formed, grows and melts back to liquid. When you think about water, think about constant change, constant transformation.

Oceanic

Over 96 percent of the water on Earth is salt water, filling the oceans and coastal marshes, caressing beaches with its waves. The oceans cover 72 percent of the Earth's surface and are themselves the most massive geophysical feature on the planet. Their average depth is over twelve thousand feet.[3] They range in depth from ankle-deep to nearly seven miles, where the pressure is eight tons per square inch—the same weight as if one person were trying to hold up fifty jumbo jets.[4] During a deep sea-dive in a submersible that descended to the ocean's deepest regions, researchers looking out the tiny portal in their thick-walled steel pod were startled to see a fish, adapted to the abyss, swimming calmly past, withstanding pressures that would have instantly crushed a human being to death.[5]

In addition to mind-bending pressure, the oceans also teem with life. Oceans provide 99 percent of the Earth's living space, and represent the largest-known space in our universe inhabited by living organisms.[6] According to the Census of Marine Life, a remarkable scientific collaboration during the 2000s to find new forms of ocean life, there have been approximately 250,000 marine species identified in scientific literature. Best estimates are that another 750,000 marine species remain to be found. There are likely upward of a billion different types of microbes living in the ocean,[7] with almost 38,000 microbes living in an average liter of seawater.[8]

Every time scientists have the resources to look, they find more ocean life forms. During the Census' Gulf of Maine Area Program in the 2000s, researchers identified two thousand new underwater species, doubling the previously known total.[9]

The diversity of these various life forms, and their ability to survive in challenging circumstances, is amazing. An article in the *L.A. Times* summarizing some of the Census' findings conveyed the strange appearances, robustness, and the life-force that characterizes sea creatures.[10] Reporter Bob Drogin noted that some tuna "commute" across the Pacific Ocean, from Los Angeles to Japan, three times per year. A seabird, a member of an endangered Albatross species, flew around the entire globe in an extended sprint of forty-six days. Coral reefs contain so many different life forms that they are referred to as "the tropical rainforests of the ocean," home to over a quarter of the world's fish species.[11] In addition to the aforementioned myriad newly discovered microbial life forms, Census explorers discovered thousands of species that live in the deep ocean, under coal-dark, frigid, pressurized conditions. These creatures, such as "manhole-sized starfish and sea spiders as big as dinner plates," engender a powerful awe at the ability of life to adapt, to survive, to exist. And even after a decade of intensive study, mysteries concerning the ocean still abound. For example, on rare occasions, portions of the ocean as large as the state of Connecticut glow at night, like a scene straight out of *20,000 Leagues Under the Sea*. It's believed that the cause may be bioluminescent microbes.[12] No one actually knows why. Census co-founder Jesse Ausubel put it well when he said, "in the end the beauty of the ocean is what inspires us."[13]

But beauty is far from the ocean's only value. Economists are increasingly able to quantify the economic value of the "ecosystem services" that the seas provide to people, services that people would have to pay for if the oceans didn't exist. Coral reefs alone provide an estimated $172 billion annually in services such as food, wastewater treatment, protection from severe weather events, and tourism.[14] Fishing's annual economic contribution to the world's economy is approximately $225 billion. The Food and Agriculture Organization of the United Nations reports that one billion people, mostly in the developing world, depend on fish as their primary source of animal protein. Over two hundred million people rely on fish and seafood-related industries for work.[15] Protecting oceans' well-being is about economic as well as environmental stewardship. And it is not an overstatement to refer to the ocean as, literally, priceless. No amount of money could purchase anything approaching a substitute.

Fresh

Fresh water represents only 2.5 percent of the world's water supply. This fresh water is ancient. The water that we drink each day has been on the earth for hundreds of millions of years, and has cycled through the atmosphere, land, plants, animal bodies, our bodies, over and over and over again.

But even this modest 2.5 percent is not all available for our use, as most of it is trapped in glaciers and ice fields, leaving only 0.007 percent of all the water on earth available for the over seven billion people on earth.[16] If all of the world's water were to fit into a gallon jug, the fresh water available for us to use would equal approximately one tablespoon.[17]

Ponds and Lakes

A lake is the landscape's most beautiful and expressive feature. It is earth's eye; looking into which the beholder measures the depth of his own nature.

—Henry David Thoreau

Ponds and lakes represent one form in which freshwater is found. Life in ponds and lakes occurs in three different zones within a given water body. At the immediate surface level, there's an abundance of life, including algae, aquatic plants, snails, clams, insects, crustaceans, fishes, and amphibians. Turtles, ducks, and snakes find their food in this part of ponds and lakes. The second zone of lakes and ponds—the near-surface level—is home to the plankton that is the foundation of the aquatic food chain. Below this is the profundal zone, where there is no light and where, because of its distance from the surface, the temperature stays fairly constant year-round.

The majority of the world's lakes and ponds are found in northern parts of the northern hemisphere, with Canada as home to the largest number of lakes of any country on the planet, with more than two million. The Great Lakes of North America are the world's largest freshwater lake system, containing more than a fifth of the entire world's surface freshwater supply. Only the polar ice caps contain more.[18] Lakes and ponds boast an array of life-forms as diverse as their oceanic and riverine counterparts, ranging from microscopic algae to fish such as North America's White Sturgeon, which can reach a length of over twenty feet.

Veins, Rivers, and Nurseries of the Planet

Rivers and streams represent a second form in which freshwater is found. *National Geographic* describes these as the "veins of the planet,"[19] sustaining ecosystems that support thousands of species and fisheries worth billions of dollars. Rivers are fed by watersheds, the land areas that serve as the catchment basin from which rainwater drains into rivers. Healthy rivers and healthy watersheds sustain enormous amounts of life.

River flows irrigate hundreds of millions of cropland annually. The rich sediment that flows naturally along rivers is a source of nutrients that keep fields productive. The diversity of river life is as astounding as that found in the oceans. *National Geographic* publishes a "Freshwater Species of the Week" on its website; recent entries have included river creatures ranging from a several-inches-long Mexican cavefish that lives in the dark with no eyesight to an Amazonian river fish that can grow to ten feet and 440 pounds to the Mata Mata turtle that is almost indistinguishable from a piece of rugged tree bark and that can breathe through a narrow, strawlike snout. Rivers and streams host an amazing panoply of life.

And they represent a great joy to people, as reflected in this short description of California's Carmel River from John Steinbeck's *Cannery Row*. "The Carmel is a lovely little river. It isn't very long but in its course it has everything a river should have. It…tumbles down a while, runs through shallows,…crackles among round boulders, wanders lazily under sycamores, spills into pools where trout live.…In the winter, it becomes a torrent,…and in the summer it is a place for children to wade in and for fishermen to wander in."[20]

Wetlands

Wetlands, formerly known by their simpler names of marshes or swamps, represent the third form in which fresh water is found—though saltwater marshes are also common. Freshwater marshes, which occur alongside or near many rivers and streams, are among the most biologically productive ecosystems on the planet. They support a level of life far out of proportion to their size while helping filter and clean excess nutrients and certain forms of pollution from rain and storm water runoff. Saltwater marshes, which occur in coastal areas and at the intersection of streams, rivers, and the ocean, support a similar abundance of life, play a similarly important filtering role, and buffer coastal communities from surging storm waters. Tidal marshes provide a home and food for clams, crabs, juvenile fish, and migratory birds. Upward of three quarters of fish species spend their early lives in the protected areas of saltwater marshes,[21] making these sites the de facto daycare centers for ocean life.

Subterranean

The final form in which water is found is underground, in aquifers. As rain falls, and as water flows across land, much of the water is absorbed into the soil. Some of this water remains near the surface and is reabsorbed by plants. The rest of the water continues its downward journey, eventually gathering in an underground, water-saturated area of sand, rocks, and gravel. These aquifers serve as important sources of water for drinking, irrigating crops, and watering animals. Aquifers generally recharge slowly, as we'll learn later. The world's largest aquifer is believed to be the Ogallala Aquifer, which underlies eight US states stretching from South Dakota to Texas. This aquifer supplies the water for crop irrigation throughout the High Plains and much of the Midwestern US, and is one main reason that this area has remained so agriculturally productive. The Guarani aquifer system underlies parts of Argentina, Brazil, Paraguay, and Uruguay, and provides much of the drinking water for almost fifteen million inhabitants.[22]

Water, Water Everywhere

It's important to think about water not only in the form of oceans, rivers, lakes, and aquifers, but also in the ways in which it is used. The amount of water used to support our daily lives, though largely invisible to us, is stunning. For example, growing a single serving of lettuce requires approximately six gallons of water. This seems like a lot until one considers that more than 2,600 gallons are required to produce a single serving of steak. An eight-ounce glass of milk requires almost fifty gallons of water to produce, which includes water for the cow and her food, plus processing-related water usage.[23] A cotton T-shirt requires more than 700 gallons.[24]

In addition to these water uses, the average US household uses close to three hundred gallons of water daily. Our biggest uses of water are flushing the toilet (27 percent of the water used by the average US household), washing clothes (21 percent), taking showers (17 percent), and using kitchen and bathroom faucets (16 percent). A stunning 14 percent of water is lost to leaks.

In reality, our daily lives are drenched with a wet overabundance. Without water, we would have almost nothing.

Waste Not

Wasted water isn't limited to leaky pipes and faucets. Because of the amount of water involved in food production, wasted food means wasted water. Columbia University reported that "in the U.S., almost half the food supply worth over $48.3 billion is lost each year, which amounts to wasting 10.5 trillion gallons of water—

enough to meet the water needs of 500 million people."[25] That's more than one and one half times the entire US population.

Six Threats

Water makes life possible. Its life-sustaining power coupled with its beauty make it one of God's greatest gifts. However, water quality faces severe threats globally. The amount of water available for human use is shrinking. And the combination of water pollution and climate change is turning water from life-sustaining blessing to primordial threat.

Waters around the world face six primary threats. Some of these are specific to the oceans, while others affect salt and fresh water bodies, and the human and biotic communities that rely on them.

1. Wanted: Dropping Acid

Ocean acidification represents the first of these threats.[26] As humanity has poured more carbon dioxide (CO_2) into the atmosphere by burning fossil fuels, the oceans have absorbed more of this gas. When CO_2 reacts with sea water, it creates carbonic acid, which inhibits the ability of many sea creatures to build the shells that they require to live. More carbonic acid means that coral reefs bleach out and die. Not only does this weaken the food chain that supports billions of fish and over a billion people. As reefs die, they can no longer protect coastal areas from severe storms, exposing vulnerable coastal communities globally to danger.

Over a quarter of the world's coral reefs have been destroyed, due in large part to ocean acidification. Only a solution to climate change will slow this deadly trend.

2. Hot Water

The warming of the ocean, again caused by climate change, represents a second threat. As the oceans warm, one result is stronger, more damaging storms, as shown by the fact that since the 1970s, the number of category four and five typhoons (the most powerful storms) has increased significantly.[27] This poses a real threat to coastal communities and results in the loss of infrastructure, property, and life. Warmer oceans also means that fish habitats change, with fish moving north to remain in the relatively cooler waters to which they are accustomed. This again represents a danger to those coastal regions that rely on fishing for sustenance and survival, communities that can't so easily "up and go" to a cooler climate to keep up with the fish. Again, a strong response to the climate crisis represents the only solution to this problem.

3. Dead Zone

As the use of fertilizers has increased globally, in combination with sewage and industrial runoff, many waters around the globe have become overenriched with nutrients. This leads to a bloom of algae which, eventually, sucks the oxygen, and the life, out of affected waters. As one research center puts it, "Habitats that would normally be teeming with life become, essentially, biological deserts."[28] In 2010, runoff from fertilizer that flowed into the Gulf of Mexico was responsible for a dead zone there the size of New Jersey.[29]

There are now more than five hundred known dead zones across the global ocean and hundreds of thousands of inland lakes and waterways where polluted runoff has choked water-born life to death. The answer? More efficient use of fertilizers, combined with innovations in crop fertilization and waste and runoff management.

4. Rising Tides

Sea-level rise, caused by a warming climate that melts polar ice while also causing seawater to expand (as water gets warmer, it occupies a larger area), represents another ocean-related danger—both to people and to coastal ecosystems. Over three quarters of a billion people around the globe live at an altitude of ten meters above sea level or less, meaning that rising sea levels plus increased severe storms place them increasingly in harm's way. And, as sea levels rise, certain freshwater supplies become undrinkable due to saltwater intrusion. Coastal Africa and South Asia, along with Pacific Island and Caribbean nations, are at greatest risk; some island nations will, within the coming century, become uninhabitable. The Alliance of Small Island States (AOSIS), a coalition of small island and low-lying coastal countries, reports that its member states constitute 20 percent of the UN's membership.[30] With members ranging from the Bahamas, Haiti, and Cuba to the Federated States of Micronesia, this community of nations includes fully 5 percent of the world's population.

In addition to threatening people living close to sea level, rising sea levels also threaten the habitats of many coastal species due to flooding and its related erosion, or full submergence. In the coming decades, the term _beachfront_ will gain a more ominous connotation than it currently holds.

5. Water Pollution

There are many forms of water pollution. Decades ago, an iconic image that symbolized water pollution would have been a drain pipe spewing contaminated waste into a river or the ocean. These kinds of discharges have been significantly reduced in the US. Today, water experts refer to "nonpoint source pollution" as a primary source of water contamination.

This kind of pollution is created when rainwater, or melting snow, moves over the surface of the ground, and seeps into the earth. This runoff picks up various chemical residues, from fertilizers, pesticides, and herbicides, and other agricultural and industrial chemicals. Eventually, these chemicals find their way into bodies of water. Cumulatively, the impact of this can be large. A Smithsonian travelling exhibition a number of years ago showed that a city of five million people may produce as much oily runoff each year as a major oil tanker spill.[31] Five quarts of oil, the amount used in a routine oil change, can contaminate a million gallons of fresh water.[32] An important part of protecting clean water supplies will involve all of us learning new ways to prevent our piece of the "nonpoint source" pie of pollution.

This isn't to suggest that industrial sources of water pollution are a relic of the past—far from it. China, for example, has hundreds of unregulated discharges of highly toxic chemicals into waterways and the ocean. A recent satellite photo over the coast of southeastern China, a center for the production of children's clothing, showed that the ocean was blackened with wastewater from a nearby city's industrial sector.[33] When it comes to toxic contamination of water, we're all on the hook—consumers and industry alike.

6. Used and Abused

A final threat facing the world's water supplies and fisheries are that they are simply overused. A number of key aquifers around the world are being depleted; it is well-recognized by experts that in many regions of the world, we cannot continue to use water as we currently are in these areas of Asia and North America without running the aquifers dry. More efficiency with water in all its uses, from agriculture to industry to households, is both possible and imperative. We can't get started soon enough.

The UN's Food and Agriculture Organization reports that 85 percent of the world's fish stocks are either "fully exploited, overexploited, depleted or recovering from depletion."[34] As populations grow, particularly in developing countries, the stress on these fisheries will also rise.

When pushed beyond their limits for too long, fisheries can and do implode. For centuries, the cod fishery off New England and Newfoundland seemed inexhaustible. Then, in 1992, after years of overuse, the fishery collapsed. Forty thousand people lost their jobs almost overnight, including ten thousand fishermen. To this day, the fishery has not approached full recovery.[35] This collapse represented an economic, humanitarian, and environmental catastrophe for a region. It demonstrates vividly how those three spheres of life are inextricably intertwined.

The long-term sustainability of the world's fish populations will depend on an intelligently designed set of regulations such as the development of sustainable catch limits and incentives such as individual fishing quotas, along with robust enforcement of these. A path to a sustainable future is visible—but not yet close to being achieved.

Land

The earth has: a solid inner core of dense iron and nickel; a liquid outer core, also of iron and nickel, ranging from 8,000 to 11,000 degrees Fahrenheit; an eighteen-thousand-mile-thick rock mantle that flows like liquid in ultra-slow motion; a rocky crust that's three to thirty miles thick and whose temperature rises over 400 degrees as it descends to the underlying mantle; and then, on top of it all, the "biologically excited layer of the Earth's crust"[36]—soil.

Soil consists of the worn-down remnants of rocks and minerals, the decomposing remains of dead plants, animals, and microbes, and of living creatures, water, and a certain amount of gaseous vapors. At the very top edge of the soil is a narrow mantle two to eight inches thick. Plants set their roots and obtain most of their nutrients from this thin slice of earth. Water is stored and purified as it passes through it. Enormous numbers of microorganisms make it home, and in turn make it possible for other plants and animals to make earth home. Topsoil, the outer layer of the skin of the planet, represents another miracle of life. "Soil is a living material," says Professor John Crawford of the University of Sydney. "If you hold a handful of soil, there will be more microorganisms in there than the number of people who have ever lived on the planet."[37] And there's not an inexhaustible supply of land that can be used for agricultural purposes; less than 12 percent of the earth's surface is currently used for this purpose,[38] and most experts project future increases in agricultural yield coming from increasingly intensive forms of agriculture with relatively modest increases in the amount of cultivated land.[39] As Mark Twain said, "Buy land, they ain't making any more of it."[40]

Miracle-Grow

Emerging from the soil, between 300,000 and 315,000 species of plants are believed to exist, providing most of the world's oxygen, producing most of the food consumed by animals and people, and having served as the source of most of the clothing, building materials, medicines, and most other building blocks of human civilization for millennia. From this overall universe of plant life, approximately seven thousand species have been cultivated for human consumption. Amazingly, today thirty crops are responsible for 95 percent of human food energy intake, with four crops—potatoes, rice, maize, and wheat—making up over 60 percent of our food-based energy intake.[41] We rely for our daily bread on a very small percentage of the overall number of forms of plant life that have ever lived on earth. This narrowing of plant diversity creates a double-edged vulnerability, because living systems with more forms of life are more resilient, more able to survive challenging changes in circumstances, than ecosystems with only a few different life forms. Think of the impact of a new pest that could devastate one of the world's four major crops—hundreds of millions of people would be affected. And think of a future with a warmer climate, when a healthy diversity of plant life will provide a range of options for living well on a hotter planet. Seed banks, which strive to preserve the diversity of plant life, are vital assets for our future. They are also chronically underfunded.

As with oceanic and animal life, plant life comes in a riotous variety of forms. In addition to hundreds of fruits and vegetables that most people have never heard of, plants range widely in size. The smallest plant is a form of duckweed that is smaller than a single ice cream sprinkle and weighs the same as two grains of salt while boasting the world's smallest fruit.[42] Most people think of trees such as a redwood or sequoia as the world's largest plants, with specimens topping three hundred feet in height and twenty-five feet in base diameter, and weighing more than sixteen times than most blue whales—the largest mammals.[43] But there are other ways besides simple height to think of the size of plants. A grove of aspen trees in Utah, nicknamed Pando (Latin for "I spread"), is connected by an underground root system with forty thousand tree trunks that emerge from the ground. Each of these trunks is genetically identical, demonstrating that Pando is a single organism. Pando covers an area of one hundred six acres. At over thirteen million pounds, it is the heaviest living organism on the planet. Pando's roots are estimated to be over eighty thousand years old.[44]

Dirt at Risk

In the face of this remarkable fecundity, our narrative about plants takes a now-familiar turn in an ominous direction. Because of various unsustainable farming methods and the growing demands we place on the soil, over 40 percent of the world's topsoil is either degraded or seriously degraded, with scientists warning that at the present rates of depletion, we have fewer than sixty years of topsoil left.[45] From overplowing and overgrazing to the overuse of certain fertilizers to the withdrawal of carbon from the soil, global agricultural practices mistreat the soil, badly. Impoverished soil can't hold water as well as healthy soil, which leads to more runoff and landslides, and which only worsens the situation.[46] We need a global agricultural reformation that invests in the healing of soil, and that maximizes the production of food that's genuinely healthy for people, unlike the unwise, unproductive subsidies showered onto corn producers and described in a *New York Times* article titled "The Great Corn Con."[47]

And it's important to remember that there are thousands of endangered plants which, while not used for human consumption, represent a vital part of the web of life. The International Union for Conservation of Nature, one of the leading global environmental organizations, maintains its authoritative Red List of threatened, vulnerable, endangered, and extinct plants and animals.[48] Between 90,000 and 144,000 plant species are estimated as being at risk of dying out, between 22 and 47 percent of the total number of species.[49]

Beasts

Mammals have backbones, hair, warm blood, and produce milk. The smallest mammal—the hog-nosed bat—weighs one twentieth of an ounce. The largest, the blue whale, is one hundred feet long and weighs 150 tons.[50] Over five thousand mammal species roam the planet.

Birds, like mammals, are warm-blooded, with wing bones that resemble rearranged versions of the human hand. Emerging from eggs that are incubated by their parents, birds are earth's only creatures with feathers, which are made of keratin—the same substance that makes up human hair and fingernails. More than ten thousand bird species have been found.[51]

The world's more than ten thousand reptile species[52] all have backbones, scales, cold blood, and lungs.[53] Amphibians—such as frogs, salamanders, and toads—also have backbones and cold blood, and breathe through their skins.[54] Over seven thousand amphibian species have been identified, most of them frogs and toads.[55]

There are nearly a million species of insects, which each have antennae and multiple legs. They hatch from eggs and have no backbone, relying on their hard exoskeletons to hold their body in shape.[56] Spiders and scorpions, which are counted as part of the arachnid order and are not insects, add another hundred thousand species to the overall list.

Welcome to the animal kingdom.

Unbelievable

Animals demonstrate a literally incredible range of attributes and abilities. Cheetahs can spot their prey from a distance of three miles.[57] Humpback whale songs, which can last up to thirty minutes, may travel ten thousand miles through the ocean waters.[58] Many scientists now recognize that elephants experience and express joy, anger, grief, compassion, and love.[59] A mosquito flaps its wings five hundred times each second.[60] The more we learn about the animal kingdom the more incredible it is revealed to be. Thanks to amazement and understanding, the distance between us shrinks.

"Barometer of Life"

But, sadly, it is not only the incredible gifts that animals offer that we must recognize but also the rapidly deteriorating circumstances in which animals of all kinds presently find themselves. The aforementioned International Union for Conservation of Nature (IUCN) Red List of threatened and endangered species is referred to as a "barometer of life,"[61] a measuring stick by which we can see the status of our fellow animal travelers on this planet. The barometric readings are sobering. In 2013, IUCN reckoned that 25 percent of all mammals are threatened, 13 percent of all birds, and a shocking 41 percent of all amphibians.[62] All of these percentages have risen by at least 20 percent since the late 1990s, indicating that we are headed in the wrong direction. As the World Wildlife Fund says, human population growth, human consumption levels, and wildlife trade have led to "an overall fall in (wildlife) population trends of 27% between 1970 and 2005." "We have picked, logged, plucked and hunted the animals, trees, flowers and fish for medicine, souvenirs, status symbols, building materials and food. And this over-exploitation . . . is currently totally unsustainable."[63]

Undervalued Asset, Intrinsic Value

When asked about the importance of protecting biodiversity, most scientists provide two types of reasons. The first reason can be described as "enlightened self-interest." In other words, protecting biodiversity of plant and animal life, and the habitat that supports these life forms, creates tremendous benefits for humanity. Biodiversity advocates point to the medicines that have been developed from plant and animal sources, and the greater security to our food supply that a diverse range of plant life provides. They also note the invaluable benefits provided by intact ecosystems. In the 1990s, for example, New York City was faced with the challenge of meeting requirements for cleaner water, and had two ways that it could meet these requirements. It could spend $6 billion to build filtration plants and $300 million annually to operate these plants. Or, it could spend $1 billion over ten years to protect the watersheds that are the source of the city's water.[64] The decision was a no-brainer.

A second reason offered for the protection of biodiversity is that it is, intrinsically, right. Esteemed conservation biologist David Ehrenfeld has written, "The non-humanistic value of communities and species is the simplest of all to state: they should be conserved because they exist and because this existence is itself but the present expression of a continuing historical process of immense antiquity and majesty. Long-standing existence in Nature is deemed to carry with it the unimpeachable right to continued existence."[65] Others extend this argument further, noting that while a vast majority of species go extinct over the long sweep of history, humanity is the cause of an equally vast majority of all present extinctions, representing an unjust intrusion into natural processes.[66]

These two reasons are complementary, not competitive. Both are compelling, in their own way. Together, they represent the cornerstones of our commitment to the protection of life.

Air

Fifty-two miles.

Over a quarter of all US citizens commute that distance to and from work. Every day.[67]

It's also the height of earth's atmosphere. This fifty-two miles contains the mixture of gases that we call air. As NASA notes, if the earth were a basketball, the atmosphere would be the thickness of a layer of plastic wrap.[68]

This seemingly flimsy band protects us from ultraviolet radiation that would fry our skin and meteors that would make earth's surface as pockmarked as the moon. It regulates earth's temperature—not too cold at night, not overly warm during the day.

Because of air pressure, 80 percent of all air is found within eleven miles of earth's surface. Humans can't survive for long at an altitude of over five miles. There isn't enough oxygen to keep us conscious.

We live in a narrow, gaseous envelope that's five miles wide. Our airliners take us higher for a few hours at a time, for a short peek above the clouds. Otherwise we exist within that narrow window.

Every Breath You Take

Air is made up of several basic component gases. Seventy-eight percent of air is nitrogen. Twenty-one percent is oxygen, which our bodies ingest through our lungs and which our cells transform into energy. A bit less than 1 percent of air is water vapor. An equivalent amount is argon, a largely inert gas whose name comes from the Greek word that means "lazy" or "inactive."[69]

And approximately 0.04 percent of air—four hundred parts per million—is carbon dioxide. Remember this.

Air Pollution—As Old as Dirt

While air pollution has become a major human and environmental health threat today, it has been recognized for centuries as deleterious to human health.

The great medieval rabbi and physician, Moses Maimonides, in addition to numerous biblical commentaries, also wrote his "Treatise on Asthma," first published eight hundred years ago. He noted that "city air is stagnant, turbid and thick.... Living quarters are best located on an upper floor.... Toilets should be located as far away as possible from living quarters.... The concern for clean air is the foremost rule in preserving the health of one's body and soul."[70] And, using ice core samples, scientists have determined that as far back as 100 BCE, the combination of metalworking and large-scale livestock operations from the Roman Empire and China's Han Dynasty created a small spike in global levels of methane in the atmosphere.[71] Even in premodern times, we had a real, if modest, impact on the atmosphere.

As the Industrial Revolution, powered by coal, got underway, air pollution increased and quality in Europe's industrializing cities worsened. London had some of the planet's dirtiest air. Despite modest legislative efforts to address London's widely recognized problem, its air quality continued to decline, into the twentieth century. Then on December 4, 1952, the Great London Smog settled over Britain's capital, bathing the city and its residents in high concentrations of smoke and sulphur dioxide.[72] One hundred thousand people were sickened. Four thousand people died as a result. Cows were reported to have choked to death in nearby fields. Within the next several years, Great Britain passed its Clean Air Act. A similar incident had taken place in 1948 in Donora, Pennsylvania, twenty-five miles outside of Pittsburgh. A heavy, industrial smog killed twenty people and sickened over a third of the town's fourteen thousand residents—a shockingly high rate. A decade after the Donora smog, mortality rates in the town were far higher than surrounding areas.[73] Nearly a quarter century later, in 1970, the US government passed the Clean Air Act, to prevent more Donora's from happening in the future.

There have been many improvements in air pollution control, and many reductions since the days of Donora. But sadly, the problem is far from solved. A 2013 study from the Massachusetts Institute of Technology found that air pollution causes two hundred thousand premature deaths annually in the United States alone. In Baltimore, the study found that 130 out of every 100,000 residents die in any given year due to long-term exposure to air pollution.[74] Globally, a World Health Organization study released in 2014 reported that a staggering seven million people died in 2012 from air pollution, with 3.7 million of these deaths due to outdoor air pollution and 4.7 million due to indoor air pollution.[75]

What's Up?

For many years, environmental scientists focused much of their attention on six primary air pollutants: ozone, particulate matter, carbon monoxide, nitrogen oxides, sulfur dioxide, and lead.[76] Each of these had been proven, beyond question, to create major health impacts.

Ozone exacerbates a variety of respiratory illnesses, such as bronchitis, emphysema, and asthma. Particulate matter (a.k.a. soot) is a mix of tiny particles and water drops that consist of various acids, chemicals, metals, and soil or dust particles, many of which are ten millionths of a meter (microns) in diameter or less. (For comparison's sake, human hair ranges from forty to one hundred twenty microns in diameter.) These particles frequently pass through the throat and nose and enter the lungs, where they affect the heart and lungs and cause serious health effects including lung scarring, lung cancer, and heart disease.

Carbon monoxide, an odorless gas that is a by-product of combustion engines, reduces the delivery of oxygen to the human heart. Nitrogen oxide and sulfur dioxide both contribute to the creation of particulate matter and ground-level ozone (nitrogen oxide). But these pollutants, which result from burning fossil fuels and a range of other industrial processes, also harm the respiratory system and increase the incidence of asthma attacks, among other negative impacts.

Lead, which was most commonly found in gasoline and paint until the early 1980s, represents one of the most toxic forms of pollution. Ingested lead affects the brain and nervous system, the kidneys, immune system, reproductive and developmental systems, and the cardiovascular system. Lead exposure is particularly devastating to children, who can develop brain damage and related behavioral problems as a result of overexposure to lead. A growing body of research has linked lead exposure to higher violent crime rates,[77] and noted that "a large portion of the decline in the US violent crime rate between 1992 and 2002 may be attributable to reductions in gasoline lead exposure."[78]

While lead poisoning's incidence has been reduced by more than 90 percent since 1980, lead still represents a significant health threat, particularly for poor and vulnerable communities. The World Health Organization reports that six hundred thousand children suffer damage to their cognitive functioning due to lead exposure.[79] Again, many of these are among the world's poorest children.

Scrubbed Clean

In the midst of these daunting figures, it's important to remember that the problem of air pollution can be solved. The air in cities from London to Los Angeles is cleaner than it was fifty years ago, thanks to a combination of better laws and regulations that forced businesses, households, and government alike to clean up their acts. From installing "scrubbers" that remove air pollution from air emissions to requirements for cleaner fuel, important progress has been made. This has been good for the economy—a 2010 study showed that a single provision of the Clean Air Act had created two hundred thousand jobs over the previous seven years.[80] As noted earlier, it's also been good for people's health. In 2010 alone, for example, this same law prevented over three million missed school days by children who would have gone to the emergency room with asthma or respiratory distress,[81] but who were spared due to cleaner air.

If the bad news is that air pollution still creates too much damage, the promising news is that the problem can be solved—if we can marshal the cultural and political will.

Four Hundred Millionths

As mentioned above, carbon dioxide currently makes up four hundred millionths of the volume of air. It seems like a small amount, until one considers its role and its historical levels.

Carbon dioxide helps keep us alive. At certain concentrations, it serves to insulate the earth like a blanket, keeping just enough warmth inside our atmosphere to allow life to flourish. But CO_2 is a powerful insulator. Too much of it, as we are learning, leads to disastrous results.

At the dawn of human civilization, the atmosphere contained approximately 275 parts per million of CO_2. As human societies developed, this level stayed relatively consistent over millennia. Human beings caused a certain level of greenhouse gas emissions by burning wood and certain other activities, but these emissions were absorbed by "carbon sinks," natural features that absorb CO_2 such as forests and oceans. But in the 1800s, the Industrial Revolution began, powered by the burning of coal. All of a sudden, human beings were taking large amounts of carbon dioxide, which had been stored underground for millions of years, and releasing this into the atmosphere. Imagine the sky, the atmosphere, as a large ocean into which we began to pour CO_2 and other gases in large amounts starting two centuries ago.

For a while, this made little appreciable difference. The sky seemed limitless and initially it was inconceivable that we could affect the temperature on a global scale. But CO_2 levels climbed relentlessly. They topped three hundred parts per million in the 1920s. In 2013, for the first time in over three million years,[82] CO_2 concentrations topped four hundred parts per million. They continue to increase at a rate of two parts per million annually. The overall trend is unmistakable.

Four hundred parts per million may not sound like much, until one considers the scientific consensus. Over the past decade, scientists have determined that 350 parts per million is the highest sustained level of carbon dioxide in the atmosphere that is "safe." James Hansen, a leading climatologist, was the first to identify this threshold. "If humanity wishes to preserve a planet similar to that on which civilization developed and to which life on Earth is adapted," he wrote, "CO_2 will need to be reduced from [current levels] to at most 350 ppm."[83]

Severe

In recent years, as the incidence of severe storms, droughts, and other extreme climate-related events has increased, more and more people have found themselves affected by our changing climate and have begun to realize what it means. In short, climate change that results from a consistent CO_2 concentration of over 350 parts per million will create devastation. Rising temperatures and sea levels, punishing storms, droughts, and floods will displace and endanger billions of people. Many will lose their lives. Many others, particularly the poorest, will lose their livelihoods and homes. Christian Aid, a relief agency, has estimated that 250 million climate refugees will exist by 2050.[84] Human society and the Earth's ecosystems will be left to future generations in tragically diminished condition, with only costly prospects for partial repair.

Our Carbon Budget

There's another way to view the challenge that climate change represents. It's widely accepted that humanity has a "carbon budget," the amount of CO_2 that we can afford to emit without forcing a reckless change in our climate. In 2013, scientists calculated that humanity could afford to emit approximately five hundred more gigatons (a gigaton is a billion tons) of CO_2 emissions before forcing the climate past the gravely dangerous threshold of a two-degree temperature rise.[85] All countries in the civilized world, ranging from Saudi Arabia to China, the United States, Australia, and all of Europe, agree that to go beyond the two-degree guardrail would endanger civilization.

Burning the proven reserves of the fossil fuel industry will create three thousand gigatons of greenhouse gas emissions, six times this threshold level.[86] At our current rate of emissions, we will surpass our global carbon budget in less than two decades.

Making It Personal

The magnitude of these numbers can make the climate crisis seem like a fearsome abstraction, a frightening advanced math problem. But for people whose lives have been altered by climate change, it's about as far from abstract as it can be.

I live in northern New Jersey, near the area that was hardest hit by Superstorm Sandy in 2012. Climatologists are insistent that it is not possible to pin responsibility for any given storm on climate change with certainty. Climatologists are equally insistent that climate change will create stronger, more frequent, more severe storms.

Like Superstorm Sandy.

During the height of the storm, when the tidal surge was at its highest, I looked out of the window of the condominium where I live and was shocked to see that my building was surrounded by water. The nearby estuary and stream had surged over its banks. The twenty-five story apartment tower had been turned into an island. It was frightening. The power of the storm was like nothing I had ever seen.

I lost power for several days, a minor inconvenience. But when I spoke to people who lived at the shore, where the storm damage had been the greatest, I heard stories of entire street blocks of houses being picked up and moved blocks away, people's homes violently transported, and wrecked, as if with the unleashed fury of an unthinkably massive force.

I heard residents of Newark, a poor city that was hit hard by the storm's flooding, talk about their apartments having been submerged by water filthy with various chemical contaminants, their living room chairs and their children's mattresses being soaked in this hazardous bath. Most people in Newark, and in many places around the world, can't afford to hire a cleaning service to scour their home after such a disaster, or to replace their basic furniture with clean, new items. So, they suffer, making due in unhealthy and dangerous circumstances that are horribly wrong.

If anything struck me most about the aftermath of the storm, it was how different it felt than all the fruitless arguments I'd witnessed over the years between climate change skeptics and those who believe it is real. These dead-end arguments represent an ideological clash. The actual aftermath of the storm felt like post-traumatic shock. People were subdued and grief-stricken, saddened and depressed. Their lives and livelihoods had taken a body blow. All of a sudden, climate change wasn't a political issue. It was human, personal.

Listen, now, to the stories of people in the developing world, dealing with the impacts of climate change. Imagine these impacts on people who have never known the level of wealth, protection, and security that we take for granted. These stories are taken from the 2014 report "Taken by Storm—Responding to the Impacts of Climate Change" from the UK-based group Christian Aid.[87]

> The waves swept everything away. Our belongings are gone. I used to make rice cakes and sell them…but now the marketplace has been washed away. —Marina Acaylan, Philippines, Typhoon Haiyan victim

> I was born here….We have problems with droughts and with landslides when the waters do come. We don't have enough water to grow our crops….People feel that they have to…leave their home to look for work and find a way of feeding their

families. —Alivio Aruquipa, Bolivia, speaking about the shrinking glaciers that previously provided water to his home community

In 2013, the *Guardian* newspaper, as part of the journalistic Climate Desk collaboration, published a series of stories entitled, "Meet America's First Climate Refugees," which detailed the challenges facing the Alaskan village of Newtok. The Yup'ik Eskimo people have lived in the region for thousands of years. Many of their villages are threatened by rising sea levels. The Army Corps of Engineers has estimated that Newtok will be underwater by 2017, and that there is no possible way to protect the village as it stands. The 350 residents of Newtok have tried, in vain, to secure funding so that their village can be moved nine miles away to a secure location. The US government, faced with similar prospects for over 150 Alaskan villages alone, has said it will not provide any funding toward the $130 million needed to move Newtok.[88]

When people of faith think about climate change, these are the kinds of stories we need to remember—multiplied millions of times over. A study from the Environmental Justice Foundation concluded that 150 million people were at risk of becoming "climate refugees" by 2050, forced to leave their homes due to the impact of climate change. Over a longer time period, the report concluded that due to climate change, 10 percent of the entire global population "is at risk of forced displacement."[89] Forget about the financial cost, which is staggering. Think about the human cost—the loss of community, the breaking apart of families, the loss of jobs. It's an unthinkable tragedy. I know it is hard to think about these things. I know it's painful. But out of compassion, out of a basic decency, out of love, we must think about them. If we don't, it calls our humanity into question.

Wedges

One useful way of envisioning a solution to climate change was articulated by the Carbon Mitigation Initiative at Princeton University, directed by Professors Robert Socolow and Steven Pacala. Socolow and Pacala sought to break the challenge of climate change into more manageable pieces by suggesting that the "world must avoid emitting about two hundred billion tons of carbon, or eight 25 billion ton wedges, over the next 50 years."[90] They proceeded to identify a number of possible "wedges," activities that could each prevent twenty-five billion tons of these emissions. The wedges are customarily grouped into categories such as "efficiency and conservation," "renewable energy and biostorage," "switching fuels," "nuclear energy," and "carbon capture and storage." Different levels of effort would be required within each of these areas in order to achieve the required emissions reductions. Most of these targets are achievable without major technological innovations. But achieving any of them, let alone eight wedges in total, will require great cultural, political, and economic change.

To date, a commitment to such change has not been forthcoming.

Tour's End

So we arrive at the end of our global tour. Admittedly, it has been short, hurried, and impressionistic, though I've tried to articulate the senses of amazement and gratitude that I believe are the proper attitudes for us to hold toward the earth, and to evoke the concern, even dread, that represent an adult appreciation of our current circumstances. The tour ends with many issues unresolved, many challenges yet unmet. And it ends with an implicit, challenging question to faith communities.

What will we do?

Discussion Questions

1. When you consider the capacity of the earth to support so many different forms of life, what are your reactions? Share these within your group.

2. Consider the list of threats facing the environment that this chapter describes. How do you react emotionally to these threats? Share your reactions within your group.

3. This chapter offers a sense of wonder at the beauty and complexity of the earth as one of God's greatest works. It also describes the serious problems with the ways we currently treat the Earth. How can your faith community bring both of these important realities to the attention of its members?

Part 3

Belief into Action

Chapter 7

A New Green Revolution

Faiths in Action for the Earth

A Presbyterian pastor stood outside at the front of a fifteen-thousand-square-foot butterfly garden, which his congregation had developed in one corner of their church's property. He closed his eyes in prayer and stretched out his arms wide open to the sky. In the moment before he spoke, a grateful smile crossed his face and an air of calm, of peace, settled among the members of the congregation. A bird called clearly in the background.

As the synagogue's energy team reviewed the numbers, they became more and more impressed. They had managed to reduce their temple's electricity usage by 30 percent and natural gas usage by 19 percent. These savings had prevented 128 tons of CO$_2$ emissions annually, equal to planting 319 trees or taking 11.2 cars off the road for an entire year. Over eighteen months, they had saved more than $50,000.

And they had done it by spending a total of $500.

Over a dozen Hindu teenagers combed the beach, picking up piles of trash. In addition to old clothes, plastic milk cartons, and aluminum cans, there were discarded devotional items from a recent Hindu festival during which people release religious items into the ocean. "This is a way to connect a new generation of Hindus with our beliefs, community service, and the protection of the Earth," said Sunita Viswanath, cofounder of Project Prithvi, which is organizing beach cleanups at New York's Jamaica Bay. Prithvi is Sanskrit for Mother Earth.

A group of fifty protestors gathered outside of the offices of the State Comptroller's office. Many of them were affiliated with secular groups advocating for fossil fuel divestment by the State of New York, the country's third largest public pension fund. A small group of people of faith stood right in the middle of the larger group, holding a sign that read,

"Divest and Reinvest Now—Religious Leaders for a Clean Energy Future." "I think we're past the point when traditional legislative advocacy can solve climate change," said one of the religious leaders. "We need to show society's leaders that we're willing to put ourselves on the line, peacefully and respectfully, but also publicly and firmly."

There is a religious revolution underway.

It is taking place on every continent, within every faith tradition.

It is changing the way people of faith experience and understand God, and what it means to live a moral life.

It is changing the ways in which people worship and pray, eat, travel, and use resources like energy and water.

It is adding a new dimension to the policy advocacy that faith communities have done for decades.

And it is drawing a small but growing number of people of faith into various forms of public witness and nonviolent civil disobedience.

The religious-environmental movement is ready for prime time.

Birth of a Movement

This movement, while it has the ancient theological roots that we've explored in this book, got its start in an on-the-ground way in the late 1980s. In 1986, the United Kingdom's Prince Philip, who was at the time President of World Wildlife Fund International, invited leaders of five major world religions, Buddhism, Christianity, Hinduism, Islam, and Judaism, to come to Assisi, Italy—the birthplace of St. Francis—to discuss how their faiths could help save the natural world. For the first time, some of the world's religious leaders met with leading environmental and conservation groups to explore how they could all work together.[1] This meeting served as a key starting point of the religious-environmental movement.

But it would be a mistake to understand the growth of this movement only from the perspective of gatherings of high-level leaders, despite their undoubted significance. From the start, grassroots faith leaders in communities around the globe, faced with local or regional environmental challenges, have understood that we must put our beliefs into action to protect the Earth.

A surprising number of these grassroots leaders found themselves, and each other, in Rio de Janeiro in 1992. There, the United Nations Earth Summit took place, and served as an opportunity for a number of key religious leaders to speak out about climate change and environmental care. Pope John Paul II, Patriarch Bartholomew, and other high-level religious leaders spoke out at or in connection with the Earth Summit, joining with political leaders in calling for action to protect the earth.

Parallel to the summit itself was a large civil society gathering, a "People's Summit." There, many of the grassroots religious activists found themselves mixed together with environmentalists, human rights advocates, indigenous people's groups, and many others. The Reverend Skip Vilas, an Episcopal priest and founding chair of GreenFaith's predecessor organization, remembers vividly how grassroots leaders from faith-based and civil society groups from around the world gathered for an overnight vigil in Flamengo Park in the middle of downtown Rio. He writes,

> We represented all of the world's religions, Eastern and Western, indigenous and modern. For several hours, as the darkness grew, we listened to talks and prayers by religious leaders and shared in the experience of music that celebrated the beauty of the Earth and the glory of Creation. Then, as night moved towards early morning, the formal meeting ended and we drifted around Flamengo Park to the tents and gathering places, where representatives of many faiths celebrated the gift of their home planet according to their own customs of prayer, music, and dance. I have always been an intellectual supporter of interfaith efforts, but that magical night in Rio spoke directly to my soul. We were there one body sharing the same religious experience of awe and deepening commitment to the Creator's call to heal the Earth.
>
> As the first light of a new day appeared above the ocean, an Australian indigenous instrument—a dijeridoo—sounded. Indigenous women were wading into the water to greet the God of the dawn. Can any doubt that the Lord of Creation loves this planet, and that we are called together as one humanity to save and heal this wonderful gift?

As I've watched the religious environmental movement grow, I've witnessed that same sense of wonder and love, of awe, gratitude, and commitment emerge from faith community after faith community. It's a powerful thing, a sign of God's realm entering our lives in a new, blessed way.

Faiths Saving Earth; Earth Saving Faiths

Emerging from the kinds of gatherings described above, the religious-environmental movement has grown consistently over the past two decades. Organizations such as the Alliance for Religions and Conservation, the Forum on Religion and Ecology, Interfaith Power and Light, the National Religious Partnership for the Environment, GreenFaith, and many more have provided important leadership. More and more faith communities have begun taking action. This increased pace of engagement shows no sign of slowing.

In the face of this growth, it's easy to assume that the storyline here is, "Faiths unite to save the planet." And while that's partly correct, it's incomplete. Over and over, religious groups that take on environmental issues find their own faith and spirituality deepened and redefined when they broaden the scope of their mission to include the environment. The story is not just about religious groups doing our part to protect the earth. It's also about our own faiths, our own images of the divine, our own understandings and lived expressions of ethics being transformed and revitalized through our focus on the earth. Faiths uniting to save the earth? Yes. The earth helping save and revitalize faiths? Yes also, in equal part.

Let's now look at the kinds of things that faith communities do when they get environmentally involved.

Spirit, Stewardship, and Justice

Religious-environmental efforts are as diverse as the monks, nuns, clergy, and lay leaders who make them happen. But generally speaking, they can be understood as falling into three basic categories. The first category, which I'll call Spirit, involves religious groups integrating the environment into activities related to worship, religious education, and spiritual practices such as prayer, meditation, and various forms of devotion. These activities represent the religious sector's spiritual and educational functions, functions this sector has carried out for millennia.

A second category of religious-environmental activity falls under the category of Stewardship. This encompasses activities related to faith communities' use and management of resources such as energy, water, food, and more.

A final category addresses the intersection of justice, equity and the environment, and includes education about the disproportionate impact that pollution has on the world's most vulnerable people and on the beyond-human community of life. This category includes activities such as education and community organizing, legislative advocacy, litigation, and forms of public witness including vigils and protests. While this feels too much like "mixing religion and politics" to some, these activities, in various forms, have been a part of the life of religious communities for thousands of years.

Let's take a look at each of these three areas.

Spirit—Worship and Ritual, Spirituality and Education

Raw and Refined—Spirituality, Ritual, and Nature

There are four ways in which faith communities are integrating environmental themes into their worship and spiritual practices. First, a growing number are increasing nature's presence during worship. For example, a recent conference cosponsored by GreenFaith and Drew Theological School included an interfaith service in which large containers of water and earth, along with native plants from local sources, were brought into the seminary chapel and placed on and around the holy table. The elements were plainly visible through the course of the service, simple, unrefined reminders of the reality of creation. This presentation of nature in a "raw" form seeks to affirm nature's intrinsic value.

Others are integrating nature into worship in a more nuanced, highly refined manner. Some have written about the importance of using local, seasonal flower arrangements and greenery, real wax candles, and locally baked bread from organic ingredients in an effort to model respect for creation while also evoking from worshippers a more sensually and aesthetically engaged experience of worship. This practice can be taken several steps further—worship bulletins printed only on 100 percent recycled paper or renewable energy credits purchased to offset carbon emissions from energy used during worship. Such a use of "refined" nature can evoke gratitude for creation's self-giving in relationship to humanity and an appreciation of ecologically and socially responsible human industry and artistry.

Ironically, technology also creates opportunities to integrate nature more deeply into worship and devotions. Many faith communities use projected images during their worship; these images can reflect environmental content in moving ways. During the interfaith service referenced above, the congregation sang a Christian hymn "God of the Sparrow," with its words edited for an interfaith assembly. The verses of the hymn were projected onto a screen, with images of nature matching the words of various verses. For instance, as the congregation sang "God of the sparrow, God of the whale," beautiful images of perching sparrows and breaching humpbacks appeared, with the hymn's text superimposed. I have also seen sound recordings of nature used during worship and devotions—bird calls, whale songs, and more. This feels weird to some, and liberating to others. It represents another way we can draw closer to creation through rituals.

Green the Tradition, Green the Pulpit

Many faith communities have begun to integrate environmental themes and references into traditional prayer forms such as calls to worship, prayers of intercession, prayers of confession, and litanies. Prayers are increasingly chosen that offer thanks for the gift and beauty of nature, that confess our sinfulness in not protecting it adequately, that express our hope for and commitment to its restoration and healing. Readings from sacred texts can be chosen, or interpreted, in a manner that speaks to environmental concerns. Music can be chosen in the same manner.

The "greening" of conventional rituals shouldn't stop with prayers, readings, and music. Sermons, or the spoken teaching offered during services of worship, can also be used to address environmental concerns. Whether through reference to the natural world as a sign of divine creativity and love, or through the prophetic engagement of issues such as climate change, clergy can use their weekly message as an opportunity to define the environment as a religious, moral concern, and to call for action on nature's behalf.

Stepping Out

Worshipping outdoors represents another way in which faith communities can deepen their connection and commitment to the earth. For urban faith communities, this may mean making use of a public park. Suburban and rural worshipping communities may have land of their own that they can use for this purpose. Outdoor worship and rituals can lead to a sacred, sensory awakening, and a deeper sense of kinship with creation. They should be part of every faith community's worship repertoire. These outdoor services do not always need to be the primary service of the week or weekend. Rather, faith communities can experiment with smaller, midweek outdoor observances at different times of day, using these to regain an awareness of nature's daily rhythms that has, largely, been lost in contemporary society.

Environmental Holy Days and Sacred Status Rituals

Religions all celebrate certain holy days, with each tradition's handful of major holidays (e.g., Easter, Yom Kippur, Diwali, Eid al Fitr) being joined by a large number of lesser religious festivals. These lesser festivals, whose meaning has often been weakened or lost over the course of time, represent a great opportunity for liturgical creativity and innovation on behalf of the environment. Over the last thirty years, the Feast of Saint Francis of Assisi, for example, has become a religious celebration of the environment, with thousands of faith communities blessing animals and even welcoming animals into the worship space on those days. (I would love to see more faith communities offering a vegetarian meal as part of this celebration, so that they refrain from eating animals on the day that they are simultaneously blessing them.) The Jewish festival of Tu B'Shvat (an ancient festival that originally celebrated the planting of trees) has become an unofficial Jewish Earth Day when rabbis' sermons frequently focus on the environment and prayers contain ecological themes. The Jewish festival of Sukkot is the fall "Festival of the Booths" during which Jewish households spend time each day in a provisional outdoor shelter. Intended to remind Jews of their dependence on God as they wandered in the desert, Sukkot has taken on strong ecological overtones, emphasizing humanity's dependence on and interconnectedness with nature. Across every tradition, opportunities abound to transform these festivals, whose meaning has become disconnected from contemporary importance, with relevant and powerful ecological themes.

God Bless You

Some religious communities have gone farther, and have reimagined some of their most central "sacred status" rituals through an environmental lens. Many religions include processes through which certain people or certain objects are connected with the divine—whether through blessings, life cycle events such as birth and marriage, or other holy designations. The boldest religious environmentalists are using this as an opportunity to assert the earth's sacredness in dynamic and arresting ways.

For eight years, GreenFaith has facilitated access to public and private financing and project management for solar energy installations for religious institutions. Each time an installation is completed, we carry out a dedication event, in which we ask for divine blessing on the solar array, and draw attention to the manner in which it generates power without air pollution or greenhouse gas emissions. When the installation is at a Jewish or Christian site, we invite a member of the congregation to read from the first chapter of Genesis. "When God began to create the heavens and the earth—the earth was without shape or form, it was dark over the deep sea, and God's wind swept over the waters—God said, 'Let there be light.' And so light appeared. God saw how good the light was. God separated the light from the darkness. God named the light Day and the darkness Night. There was evening and there was morning: the first day" (vv. 1-5).

Each time the passage is read, an amazed stillness comes over the congregation as these ancient words take on new meaning, and the congregation's use of energy takes on a sacred urgency.

There are examples from other traditions. Five times each day, Muslims pray— this is one of the pillars of Islam. In preparation for prayer, Muslims conduct *wudu*, a ritual ablution, washing their hands, face, and more to express their commitment to moral and spiritual self-purification as they bring themselves before Allah. This practice, as central to Islam as kneeling to pray is for many Christians, uses a large amount of water every day.

A growing number of Muslims are teaching restraint in the use of water during *wudu*, making reference to the global scarcity of clean water and numerous Islamic sources, dating back to the Prophet Mohammed, that represent a clear commitment to the careful and spare use of water.[2]

And, as mentioned earlier, a small number of Muslims are reviving the practice of dry *wudu*, using earth instead of water to cleanse themselves before praying. Here's how it works: A person takes a handful of earth, and uses it as he or she would use water—rubbing it over the hands and face. This Qur'an affirms this practice in the absence of water: "But if you are sick or on a journey...and you cannot find water, then make your ablution on clean ground and wipe a part of your faces and your hands. Indeed Allah is all-excusing, all-forgiving."[3] From the Hadith (the collection of sayings attributed to the Prophet Mohammed), the meaning of this affirmation is amplified: "All of the earth has been made for me and my nation a pure place of prayer. Whenever a person from my nation wants to pray, he has something with which to purify himself, that is, the Earth."[4]

I've witnessed *wudu* performed with great care with less than two cups of water, the supplicant washing hands, face, ears, feet, and mouth with expressive respect for Allah and for the water itself. I've also witnessed dry *wudu*, and was struck by the counterintuitive yet stunning epiphany that I felt watching someone make himself dirty in one sense and spiritually pure in another. I'm reminded of the Swiss psychoanalyst Carl Jung, who wrote "People get dirty through too much civilization. Whenever we touch nature, we get clean."[5]

Practice Makes Perfect

For over a decade, wilderness guide, Buddhist teacher, and Congregational minister Kurt Hoelting led meditation trips to Alaska's coastal waters. There, he taught his traveling companions the practice of outdoor meditation, which he sought to capture in his short film *Deep Presence—Meditations on a Wild Coast.* In this film, he demonstrated outdoor walking meditation, a simple mindfulness practice in which a person walks with intentional slowness, seeking to retain a focused, calm awareness while taking each step, remaining in the present moment, mindful of the rising and falling of his or her breath. Others have taught "mindful eating," in which people eat with an unhurried purposefulness, seeking to taste their food with greater awareness than is normally the case. I've led sessions in which people slowly eat fresh organic produce and the same produce from a factory farm. The difference in flavor, and then in meaning, is very real. Experienced in intentional slow-motion, it is memorable.

These two examples, of mindful walking and mindful eating, represent only a tiny portion of eco-spiritual practices designed to reconnect us with the earth and with its Source, and to awaken us to the need to care for creation more deeply. Leaders from Joanna Macy to Brian Swimme to John Seed and many others have offered examples of rituals and spiritual practices that can enchant or shock us, or both, while waking us up to the earth around us, recognizing our bond with it, and facing forthrightly its present plight. These practices, like all good spiritual practices and good rituals, resemble the chef's practice of reduction, through which flavor (in religion's case—meaning) is intensified through boiling (in religion's case—focused attention). Done properly, these rituals and practices make an indelible mark on people's souls, enabling them to access deep levels of human knowing, relating, and valuing. They are an indispensable part of a healthy spiritual life, and they will spread widely in the coming years.

The footprint of religious institutions in the areas of education, worship, and spiritual practice is massive. Regarding worship and spiritual practice, over 350,000 houses of worship in the US offer weekly worship services or religious observances.[6] There are over 220,000 Catholic parishes[7] alone around the world. Imagine the beneficial impact if, each week, billions of people around the planet prayed, or meditated, not only on behalf of themselves and of those they love but also on behalf of the earth. Such a practice could unleash a powerful flood of religious feeling, emotional connection, and moral commitment for the protection of the planet. It could be an unbelievable force for good.

Teach Me—Religious Education and the Earth

Around the world, faith-based institutions provide religious and moral instruction for children, teenagers, and adults. In these classes, people of faith learn about the rich narratives of their sacred writings. They absorb fundamental moral teachings about the love of neighbor and the dignity of life. They wrestle with the challenge of developing a mature, spiritual, moral self, and learning the skills to build loving relationships in the midst of life's complexities. They learn to engage the public issues of their time, applying ancient wisdom to contemporary urgencies.

Now, they are beginning to integrate the environment into all aspects of religious education.

Finding a Voice

The GreenFaith Fellowship Program is an eighteen-month educational experience for people of faith—clergy and laity—who want to deepen their understanding of the link between faith and the environment. During the program, the Fellows' first project is to write their eco-theology. It is based on the assumption that by examining their own experience of the sacred in nature, and their religious tradition's teachings on the environment, they can find their own authentic religious identity in relationship to the earth. They can find their own voice, in a new, green way.

The first step in the process is the eco-autobiography, a writing exercise in which Fellows reflect on the different stages of their lives—childhood, adolescence, young adulthood, adulthood, and elderhood. They think about when they have experienced God outdoors, when they've had deeply meaningful or spiritual experiences outside. After they write these down, they reflect on the themes that have emerged, threads of meaning that link the various stories they've recalled. These themes, such as awe, gratitude, wonder, community, beauty, love, and vividness, reappear over and over again.

The next stage of the eco-theology process involves examining one's own religious tradition, identifying the passages from sacred writings, the prayers, the rituals, the religious teachings that relate to the environment. Fellows learn to think about how ancient teachings, such as love for neighbor, can be extended to include our relationship with the earth, or how classical teachings about self-restraint in material consumption take on new meaning in the age of our ecological crisis. Ancient traditions come alive in new ways through this process.

When they've finished this, Fellows then identify the three or four core themes that represent their own religious-environmental identity. They name spiritual attitudes such as gratitude, respect, and awe. They name moral commitments such as reducing the environmental impact of their own consumption, conserving nature, or advocating for an environmentally sustainable society. They identify stories, from their own experience and from their tradition, that exemplify these ecological values.

This approach reflects one model of religious education on the environment. It includes spiritual self-examination, study of one's tradition, and the personal integration of the wisdom that emerges from this reflection.

Faith communities around the world help their members develop deeply held attitudes and beliefs about how they should treat other people. The process I've described here enable these same communities to help their members gain depth of identity in relation to the earth—an "ecological identity"[8] as part of our religious identity.

Seeing Is Believing

Most people don't visit pollution on purpose.

Two or three times each year, in collaboration with a community-based organization in Newark, New Jersey—the Ironbound Community Corporation—that's exactly what members of faith communities do, through a GreenFaith Environmental Justice Tour. We board a bus and take a two-hour tour through the Ironbound, a densely crowded, colorful immigrant community that is home to more than twenty thousand people. The air is filled with the sounds of a vibrant city neighborhood and the smells of Portuguese cooking from the homes and restaurants along the main streets. On the surface, the Ironbound looks like a classic American urban community, a mosaic of cultures and ethnicities engaged in their daily lives.

But, like many urban communities of color, the Ironbound is home to dangerous levels of pollution. Air pollution levels are consistently well above the federally identified safe levels, due in part to the emissions from thousands of diesel trucks that pass through the neighborhood on the way back and forth from Ports Newark and Elizabeth, the largest ports on the East Coast. Toxic fumes, euphemistically referred to as "vapor intrusions," periodically emerge from the ground into the neighborhood's homes and crowded schools, the legacy of decades of legal and illegal chemical dumping. The region's largest incinerator, which burns trash from northern New Jersey as well as much of Manhattan, spews more mercury emissions into the air than any other facility in the state. The Passaic River, which bounds the neighborhood on one side, is so contaminated that seventeen miles of it are a Federal Superfund site, the designation given to the most heavily contaminated sites. It's the largest site of its kind in the nation.

Pollution is an abstraction for many of us. But when people see the Ironbound and its environmental burdens and see that this polluted air and land impact real people living real lives, the issues, and their moral import, become equally real.

Faith communities have recognized the value of "learning by seeing," or "immersion education," for decades. When applied to the environment, this form of education offers people an opportunity to experience, albeit briefly, the moral, practical, and political challenges involved in creating an environment that's consistent with the teachings of our traditions, an environment that supports a healthy life for all people, regardless of race or income or background. By giving people a multisensory experience and the knowledge that enables them to see pollution that most people don't know how to see, these tours create rich opportunities for moral reflection for faith communities.

This kind of education doesn't need to be limited to visiting polluted sites. We've taken people on tours of "green buildings" such as the Quaker Center in Philadelphia, and watched as people learn about how an office building can use far less water through efficient toilet and faucet fixtures and by capturing rainwater for certain uses, and can reduce its carbon footprint by using natural light and geothermal energy. We've also taken people on a walk through a marsh, where they see the diversity of life that the wetlands support and learn about the threats posed by polluted runoff.

In each instance, an actual visit to an environmentally significant site serves as a powerful eye-opener, and provides people with a vision of what's right, what's wrong, and what needs to happen.

Back to School

Most members of faith communities take part in some form of religious education—whether as children, teenagers, or adults. Through this education, faith communities transmit their values and traditions, their sacred stories and customs. They offer guidance for living a morally, spiritually healthy life. They share teachings about the moral imperative to care for the poor, to protect the dignity of the most vulnerable members of the human community.

Now, a growing number of faith communities are examining their own traditions to integrate the protection of the earth into the pantheon of values that they pass on to their members. Through a range of activities like the ones described above, these communities are redrawing the boundaries that represent who and what we must care for to include the natural world. They're teaching that it's a religious obligation to protect the planet, in the same way that it is to feed the hungry.

As with worship and spiritual practices, the potential impact of religious institutions in this area is massive. According to UN Secretary General Ban ki Moon, "Together, the major faith groups have established, run, or contribute to over half of all schools world-wide."[9] The Secretary General also notes the educational impact of religious groups through their various media outlets, saying that the world's religious groups "produce more weekly magazines and newspapers than all the secular press in the European Union."[10] Religiously based environmental education, education that awakens us to the challenges facing the planet and the values that must guide our response, will be a vital part of the educational mission of faith communities in the years ahead.

Stewardship

Power Surge

When Temple Beth Rishon in Wyckoff, New Jersey, was rebuilt in 2000, the focus was on aesthetics. The temple sanctuary ceiling soars skyward, creating an inspiring space in which to pray.

Mark Neiderman and Harriett Shugarman, two members of the temple who care about the environment, thought they could make this spiritually powerful space more energy efficient. They gathered a small committee and began to track their energy usage, enabling them to quantify their greenhouse gas emissions and future energy savings. They mapped the usage of the temple complex and found ways to power down portions of the facility that were not used on a regular basis. They adjusted their temperature controls and tightened up their management of the heating and cooling equipment. They made one small financial investment in a $500 piece of equipment that made their refrigerators operate more efficiently. The results were spectacular. "After returning over $30,000 to our operating budget over a couple of years, we requested a line item in the proposed budget for $4,000 to reinvest in energy-saving improvements," said Neiderman. "The board was happy to give a green light to that investment."[11]

While not every site will enjoy the same level of success as Temple Beth Rishon, energy efficiency and conservation projects are sprouting up in faith communities nationwide—for good reason. The US EPA "estimates that if America's 370,000 congregations cut energy use just 20% it would save nearly $630 million for missions and other priorities, (and) prevent more than 2.6 million tons of greenhouse gas emissions—the equivalent of eliminating emissions from 480,000 cars, or planting 60,000 trees."[12]

Every year.

Here Comes the Sun

On a recent summer morning, members of Lord of Life Lutheran Church in the New Jersey Pinelands gathered in the sunlight outside the front of their church. Dozens of blue-black solar panels on the roof of their facility shimmered in the sun, the panels' silicon interior silently shedding electrons into an embedded grid of silver wiring that leads to a central power line. With the pastor looking on, a member of the congregation read from the first chapter of Genesis, and a blessing was pronounced over the solar array. Lord of Life now gets a significant portion of its electricity from the sun.

While solar projects for faith-based sites are difficult to finance and to negotiate, the results are, well, electrifying. That's why faith-based schools and worshipping communities nationally are looking into solar. These projects represent a visible way for faith groups to wear their environmental commitment on their sleeves (on their roofs, actually). "Years ago, if people saw solar panels on a church, they would have thought it was weird," says Reformed Church pastor Seth Kaper-Dale, whose church "went solar" through a GreenFaith program. "We think it's cool, and part of how we understand what it means to be faithful to God."

Water, Water Everywhere

"One-sixth of the world's freshwater is in the Great Lakes" said the Reverend Suzelle Lynch, minister of the Unitarian Universalist Church West in a suburb of Milwaukee. "It's a powerful issue for us here."[13]

Lynch and other religious leaders had assembled on the shores of Lake Michigan at the Interfaith Conference of Greater Milwaukee's "Making Waves for Water" event at the Milwaukee Community Sailing Center. These leaders were gathered to show their support for water conservation and water quality protection by faith communities.

The gathering also represented the Wisconsin launch of the GreenFaith Water Shield, an environmental merit badge program for faith communities through which congregations and religious schools offer prayers of gratitude for water, pray for its conservation, and take practical steps to save water and prevent water pollution. Participating groups take steps such as installing flow restrictors on their congregation's faucets and capturing rainwater to water plants and to reduce storm water runoff. They then ask their members to take simple water-saving steps at home, such as installing faucet flow restrictors, taking shorter showers, and more. Fifteen percent of the membership of a faith community must commit to taking conservation steps at home for the site to earn its Water Shield. Twenty faith communities in the greater Milwaukee area will be earning the Water Shield, impacting hundreds of households. It's a great example of how faith communities can use their presence within a community to create positive change.

Waste Not

Twenty people, ranging in age from two to sixty-two, were gathered on the grounds of the Reformed Church of Highland Park. With great pomp and circumstance, the two pastors and several members of the congregation hauled the week's trash into the center of the gathering—seven large bags, bursting at the seams. Everyone put on a pair of latex gloves, and a tarp was spread on the ground. "I went to seminary for this?" joked one of the pastors. Then, two members of the congregation ripped the trash bags open, one by one. The children squealed with simultaneous disgust and delight, and many of the adults couldn't help but crack a smile. Coffee grounds, paper plates, newspapers, cans, and bottles spilled onto the tarp. The waste audit had begun.

Church members gingerly picked through the trash, sorting it into piles of recyclables, compostable waste, and trash. After ten minutes of sorting, the results were becoming clear. Approximately one quarter of the waste could either be composted or recycled. The mountain of Styrofoam cups could be eliminated if the church switched to mugs for coffee hours. If these steps were taken, the church would reduce the volume of its trash by close to 50 percent. Not fifteen. Fifty. By creating a visually memorable tableau, waste audits serve as powerful educational activities, waking people up to the ways we can reduce the amount of trash that we create.

But in addition to reducing the amount of garbage they themselves produce, faith communities can also serve as gathering places for community members to dispose responsibly of some of the more dangerous forms of waste that many people possess. GreenFaith has organized electronic waste recycling days when local congregations partner with an electronic waste recycler and invite community members to bring their old computers, monitors, and other outdated electronics so that tons of toxic waste can be kept out of landfills. At these events, we've filled large trucks with hundreds of pieces of outdated equipment. The amount of electronic waste is growing exponentially around the world, and it contains significant amounts of chemicals and heavy metals which are dangerous to people and the planet. Much of this waste is shipped overseas where poor laborers in Africa or China disassemble it by hand, with no protection, for pennies an hour.

Proper recycling protects human health and the earth. It creates jobs. By hosting these kinds of events, faith communities can join with local governments to reduce the amount of trash we produce and protect people from the health threat it represents if it is disposed of improperly.

Food and Faith

Where else can you say a blessing while using recycled vegetable oil to fuel a truck that is filled with organic produce and naturally fermented kosher pickles? Come see for yourself![14]

—Webpage for Adamah, an organic, Jewish educational farm in Connecticut

Many environmental topics are challenging and can feel depressing because of the magnitude of the problems we face. But when the conversation turns to food, the tone of the conversation shifts. Few topics are better at lifting the spirits.

Hazon, the organization whose organic farm is mentioned above, offers a range of programs that connect the US Jewish community with opportunities to support organic farming and to enjoy delicious produce. Hazon has helped organize dozens of Community Supported Agriculture projects (CSAs) at synagogues around the country. Members of synagogues, and of the wider community, purchase a portion (a share) of the produce of a local organic farm, with the synagogue parking lot or grounds serving as the place where the farmer delivers the shares every week. By identifying the shareholders more efficiently than the farmer often could on his or her own, the synagogue plays a vital role in supporting a local organic farm. Members of the synagogue enjoy access to a variety of tasty, healthy seasonal vegetables and fruits—not normally considered to be a membership perk at a house of worship.

Many other faith communities are launching gardening projects. Some congregations use these as an intergenerational activity to connect their elders with children. Others offer garden space to members of their community, providing them with access to a plot of land where they can grow produce for themselves. Still other congregations grow fresh produce that they offer to their members and to local food pantries as a supplement to the dry and packaged goods that are provided to the hungry in the area. Grace Episcopal Church in Chattanooga not only launched a community garden, through which a number of church and community members used church land for gardening and for teaching children to grow vegetables. They also took additional care with their grounds, receiving the "Golden Acorn" award from the Chattanooga Tree Commission for their efforts, organized a farmer's market that accepted food

133

stamps and welfare benefits for payment from low-income families, and published a newsletter with cooking tips and recipes.

Body and Soul

This focus on food by faith communities can have, literally, life-saving impacts. The Body and Soul Program, sponsored by the National Cancer Institute, the American Cancer Society, the University of North Carolina, and the University of Michigan, was a response to high stomach cancer rates among African Americans. Recognizing the important role that the church plays in many black communities, researchers developed a program that sought to increase church members' fruit and vegetable intake, a proven way of decreasing the incidence of this deadly disease.[15]

Implemented in dozens of African American churches in Michigan, North Carolina, Virginia, Delaware, and California, Body and Soul included four components. After the pastor in each church made a commitment to healthy eating, participating congregations began to offer fruits and vegetables at all church functions where food was served. Church members were trained as peer counselors for fellow congregants who wanted to change their eating habits. Congregations hosted cooking classes or other educational programs to help families add fruits and vegetables to their household diet. The results were substantive and positive, with participants increasing their fruit and vegetable intake measurably. Clearly, what's good for the body and soul can also be good for the earth.

This belief is at the core of the work of Hindu monk Gadhadara Pandit Dasa, the first official Hindu chaplain at Columbia and New York University. In addition to spiritual reflection workshops and interactive discussions on the Bhagavad Gita, the Hindu spiritual classic, Pandit also offers vegetarian and vegan cooking workshops.[16] His teaching about vegetarian cooking makes the body-soul-planet connection abundantly clear, and serves as a reminder that our consumption habits carry profound eco-spiritual meaning.

Energy and water. Food and waste. These are among the most fundamental elements of human society. As we've seen, faith communities can foster ecologically healthy practices in relation to each of these. Houses of worship can equip their members not only with the spiritual teachings in their support but also, as importantly, with the practical tools and supportive community that makes it possible for people to create and sustain eco-friendly habits. Again, action at scale by religious groups would make a sizeable impact. The Catholic Church is estimated to own over 170 million acres, making it one of the world's five largest landholders, for example.[17] In the US alone, there are over 350,000 congregations.[18] If the resource use on these lands and within these facilities were made more environmentally sustainable, the results would be substantial indeed. Religious efforts would not be solely symbolic. They would be concretely real.

Justice and the Ecosphere

There's one further area in which faith communities have a vital role to play in the development of an environmentally sustainable society. In addition to worship and spiritual practice, education and consumption habits, faith communities can use their influence to advocate for environmentally protective policies by governments and corporations. Not all faith communities are comfortable playing the advocate's role. But it's undeniable that, over the centuries, religious groups have had a profound impact on the worldviews and beliefs that shape the rules that societies play by, their sense of right and wrong.

Noah's Ark 2.0

The Endangered Species Act is our Noah's Ark and Congress and special interests are trying to sink it!

—Dr. Calvin DeWitt, Professor of Environmental Studies and Evangelical Christian

In 1996, the new majority in Congress had its sights set, among other things, on the Endangered Species Act, the legislation that protects animals and plants whose habitats are in danger of disappearing. But a group of Evangelical Christians, coordinated by the Evangelical Environmental Network (EEN), had other ideas. The group organized letter-writing campaigns and waves of calls to congressional offices, demonstrating conservatives' support for the law. Facing this unexpected resistance, congressional leaders backed down.[19]

Since then, EEN has continued to build an impressive record of advocacy on behalf of people and the environment, utilizing messages that resonate with its constituency. EEN has advocated for reducing toxic power plant emissions and stronger regulation of toxic chemicals, marshaling convincing evidence that these toxins represent a threat to pregnant women and to "unborn life." EEN leader Mitch Hescox, a pastor who worked for over a decade in the coal industry, is a passionate advocate who encourages leaders to "think big" when it comes to solving environmental problems.

> I see cleaner skies and purer water, healthy children free to enjoy the beauty of God's creation, their bodies not hindered by pollution, their brains not diminished by toxics. I see an economy that is the envy of the world producing the technologies that

help us achieve life, liberty, and happiness; plentiful, affordable energy to power our homes and vehicles and businesses, freeing up time to spend with family and loved ones, to rebuild community life, and to be creative with the gifts God has given each of us.[20]

His vision is bold and unafraid. As an Evangelical with deep roots in a community that historically has been at odds with many environmentalists, his voice is a vital one.

A Climate for Change

Approximately one third of all greenhouse gas emissions in the US come from the generation of electricity by power plants. In late 2013, with the US Congress unwilling to debate legislation, the Environmental Protection Agency issued proposed standards to reduce the release of carbon pollution from these plants, creating cleaner air and a healthier environment for children and future generations.[21]

Almost immediately, certain industry groups rose in opposition. The American Petroleum Institute, a national trade association representing the US oil and natural gas industry, called the rules a regulatory "overreach," and filed a petition with the US Supreme Court challenging them.[22]

Interfaith Power and Light is a national religious response to climate change, with affiliates in thirty-eight states. IPL has advocated at the state and federal level for years in support of legislation to address climate change. When the EPA's new rules were released, the Reverend Sally Bingham, President of Interfaith Power & Light said, "We have a moral obligation to do everything in our power to protect the health of all people (and) preserve Creation.... The new EPA rules are an important first step in cutting carbon pollution and improving air quality nationwide. We aim to fulfill the call from God to be stewards of Creation, and will be championing the EPA's action in houses of worship across the country."[23] But IPL didn't stop with words. In February 2014, more than fifteen thousand IPL followers sent Valentine's Day postcards to their congressional representatives, urging them to support the new EPA rules.

These new rules face intense opposition in states where coal remains an important industry, and in certain oil-rich states. But these kinds of cultural and political struggles are an unavoidable part of the transition to a sustainable future, and faith communities have a moral obligation to be involved. As Bingham notes, "congregations have been changing lightbulbs, installing solar rooftops and geo-thermal systems and shrinking our carbon footprints for years. We've shown that it can be done. But we know that these actions alone will not be enough to turn the tide of global warming. Along with individual behavior change, we need strong policies. There's simply no other way."

Day in Court

The Essex County Resource Recovery Facility—also known as an incinerator—is located in Newark's Ironbound community, the busy immigrant community that faces numerous environmental challenges and that's featured in the environmental justice tour described earlier. Constructed despite fierce opposition in a community whose asthma rates are more than double the state average, the incinerator is the largest of its kind in the New York City area. It burns 2,800 tons of waste daily,[24] including a significant amount of waste from New York City. It also releases more mercury than any of the other four incinerators in the state.[25] Its owner and operator is Covanta, a large "waste to energy" company that operates incinerators around the US.

For years, environmental leaders at the Ironbound Community Corporation (ICC), a local community services organization, had received reports showing that the incinerator was violating its air emissions permits many times each year.[26] ICC had reached out numerous times, trying to engage Covanta in a discussion about improving the incinerator's air pollution control technology. The efforts were fruitless. Plant management did not return phone calls or respond to letters. It was as if the community group did not exist.

GreenFaith had worked for over a decade with ICC, educating clergy and religious leaders about the environmental health threats, including the incinerator, facing Newark residents. After a number of discussions with a nonprofit environmental law firm, the organizations agreed to sue Covanta in an effort to force the company to reduce its air pollution. GreenFaith had legal standing in the case because several GreenFaith members, including two Catholic nuns who ran a school in nearby Jersey City, lived in the area affected by the incinerator's emissions.

On February 20, 2009, the Eastern Environmental Law Center filed a lawsuit on behalf of ICC and GreenFaith in the United States District Court alleging that the incinerator had violated federal pollution limits concerning the emission of sulfur dioxide, carbon monoxide, and fine particulate matter on hundreds of occasions. Sister Eleanor Uhl, principal of Resurrection School in Jersey City and a resident of Jersey City, wrote in her affidavit to the court:

> I became especially concerned about the air quality in Jersey City after personally observing the respiratory problems of my students. The number of students with asthma has increased dramatically over my fourteen-year tenure. A vast number of Resurrection School students are dependent upon inhalers. Accordingly, all of the teachers receive special training to deal with asthmatic students. The physical

education teachers often must restrict outdoor physical activity of the asthmatic children. On at least one occasion, I had to call an ambulance to the school for a young boy who suffered an asthma attack after playing outside during recess.

On very hot days, I can see pollution in the air. If I open the windows to the school, I will find the table surfaces dusty and gritty as a result of the particulates in the air. Poor air quality exacerbates the children's asthma. Most of the children who must visit the nurse during school hours go for asthma-related health issues. A large majority of student absenteeism is due to respiratory illness or problems related to asthma.[27]

After years of nonresponsiveness, within one week of the suit's filing, meetings between Covanta's management and legal team, ICC, and GreenFaith had commenced.

In the following year, the litigation went nowhere. Along with our attorney and colleagues from ICC, I attended numerous meetings with Covanta's legal team and plant management, seeking a resolution. While the plant's management struck a consistently collegial tone, no settlement offer materialized. We spent hour after hour seated across the table from a bank of corporate lawyers, getting nowhere. It appeared that Covanta's plan was to try to exhaust our meager resources in the hope that we would simply go away. Otherwise, there was no rational explanation for so many wasted hours of time, let alone the legal expenses that the firm was incurring.

Finally, the judge overseeing the case pressed both sides to enter mediation. A settlement agreement began to take shape. Finally, in late 2010, the two sides agreed that Covanta would install new air emissions control technology to reduce some of the plant's harmful air pollution, seek to keep dangerous or inappropriate waste out of the incinerator, fund a mercury collection program in the surrounding area to reduce the amount of mercury burned in the incinerator, and provide $875,000 to be used for a green space recreation project in the Ironbound.[28] It was a meaningful victory that would create real benefits for the community.

Two years later, a new development emerged. In the lawsuit, ICC and Green-Faith had asked Covanta to install a piece of equipment called a "baghouse," the current standard in air pollution control technology, at the Newark incinerator. At the time, Covanta refused. In 2012, Covanta and the Essex County Executive proudly announced that the incinerator would be installing the baghouse equipment in the coming several years.[29] Their public announcement included no mention of pressure from the community playing a role in the decision. To this day, ICC and GreenFaith believe that it helped.

Many faith communities would never consider taking part in legal action to address environmental issues. But without action such as this, and without the force of law, some polluters will simply not respond. If faith communities are serious about addressing environmental injustice, they need to be willing to use the variety of tools at their disposal. Sometimes, legal action is the only way that small, community-based organizations can force large corporations to respond. It's David and Goliath all over again, in green clothing.

Divest and Reinvest Now!

By the end of 2012, environmental advocates had been conducting education on climate change for over twenty years and pressing, unsuccessfully, for national climate legislation for fifteen. The political landscape made it seem completely implausible that such legislation was forthcoming, while scientific reports noted that global emissions were rising faster than ever. Polls continued to show that most Americans did not view climate change as a priority. The situation was dire.

"Do the Math"

In the summer of 2012, environmentalist and author Bill McKibben published an article in *Rolling Stone* magazine that, unexpectedly, went viral fast. Titled "The Terrifying New Math of Global Warming," the article highlighted three numbers that made clear the gravity of the climate situation and the threat posed by the fossil fuel industry. The first number was two degrees centigrade, the highest level of temperature rise that scientists and the world's governments agreed was acceptable if catastrophic impacts from climate change were to be avoided. Governments from Saudi Arabia to the US to Europe and many others concurred. Two degrees was the absolute upper limit.

The second number was 565 gigatons. This was the amount of CO_2 that we could emit into the atmosphere before forcing the temperature past the two degree threshold. McKibben and others referred to this as our "carbon budget."[30] At current emissions rates, humankind will have used up its carbon budget within thirty years.[31]

The third number placed the first two in a compelling context by identifying the level of CO_2 emissions embodied in the proven oil and gas reserves of the fossil fuel industry, a number identified through research by the British-based Carbon Tracker Initiative. That number? Almost 2,800 gigatons of CO_2.[32] Five times our global carbon budget. It's notable that the fossil fuel industry has not challenged these well-publicized figures. It's equally reasonable to expect that the industry plans to use these reserves, since this represents its core business activity. And, the industry clearly has no plans to get out of the fossil fuel business. In 2013, it spent over $600 billion exploring for new fossil fuel reserves,[33] far beyond the $244 billion invested globally in renewable energy.[34]

A set of additional figures makes it clear that the fossil fuel industry's threat is not limited to the impact of its products, but is also expressed through its political influence. The International Energy Agency reports that fossil fuel industry receives $1.5 billion globally per day in government subsidies,[35] and spends over $400,000 per day to lobby the US government alone.[36] The industry's ability to tilt the playing field in its favor represents as grave a threat to life as do the fossil fuels themselves.

In the face of these striking figures, McKibben argued, "Given this hard math, we need to view the fossil-fuel industry in a new light. It has become a rogue industry, reckless like no other force on Earth."[37] He went on to quote Naomi Klein, a writer and activist. "Lots of companies do rotten things in the course of their business—pay terrible wages, make people work in sweatshops—and we pressure them to change those practices. But these numbers make clear that with the fossil-fuel industry, wrecking the planet is their business model. It's what they do."[38]

McKibben's article pointed to nascent efforts on college campuses to pressure these institutions to divest from fossil fuel holdings, selling the stocks and bonds in their endowments of the two hundred largest oil and gas companies. Drawing on the memory of the impact of divestment campaigns in toppling South Africa's apartheid regime, he called for a new wave of divestment, focused on fossil fuels, as a means of revoking the "social license"[39] of the industry and of making meaningful political action on climate change possible again.

Getting Organized

The argument struck a chord. Within less than a year, several hundred campus-based divestment groups had sprung up. Faith communities also began to get involved. In the summer of 2013, thanks to the leadership of the Reverend Jim Antal, the United Church of Christ voted at its national General Synod to divest from fossil fuels, a stunningly bold action. Earlier in 2013, GreenFaith had launched its *Divest and Reinvest Now! Campaign*, seeking to support faith-based divestment efforts through education, networking, and resolutions at the denominational level. Grassroots campaigning took off in numerous denominations, with groups such as the Unitarian Universalist–focused *UU Divest*, the Presbyterian Church USA–focused *Fossil Free PCUSA*, and the United Methodist–focused *Fossil Free UMC* springing into existence. America Magazine, a leading Catholic periodical, published a tightly argued piece that made the case for divestment by Catholic colleges and universities based on a range of papal and Catholic Social Teachings.[40] Prominent theologians and religious leaders signed GreenFaith's *Divest and Reinvest Now!* statement, calling not only for faith-based divestment from fossil fuels but also a reinvestment in a clean energy future. Archbishop Desmond Tutu joined in, throwing the weight of his moral authority behind the effort.[41] GreenFaith is publishing the first in its series of "edu-comics" on the topic, depicting in the form of a comic book a number of twenty-somethings from different faith traditions pressing their faith and educational institutions to divest and reinvest.

The fossil fuel divestment movement has spread rapidly, and continues to grow. In early 2014, Oxford University published a study[42] reporting that it was the fastest growing corporate campaign in history, and identifying many ways in which it could make a meaningful impact. It may well be that this campaign, combined with the increasingly urgent reports from a range of scientific authorities and the work of many activists over the decades, finally creates the conditions in which a large-scale response to climate change becomes possible.

OurVoices.net

For years, it has been widely recognized that an international treaty that requires greenhouse gas emissions reductions is vital to solving the climate crisis. In 1989, almost all major countries in the world adopted the Kyoto Protocol, an agreement designed to do just that. However, the United States, China, and Russia, three major emitters, refused to sign on. To date, there is no agreement in place.

In mid-2014, with partners in the United Kingdom, GreenFaith launched OurVoices.net, an international, multifaith campaign in support of a global climate agreement. The campaign involves an online call to action, seeking to attract the support for a climate treaty of at least one million people from around the world by the end of 2015. OurVoices.net also involves a series of days of prayer and action through which religious and spiritual communities globally show their support publicly for a climate deal. The campaign's first public prayer action was called "Solidarity Sea Prayers," and it involved people around the world standing ankle deep in the ocean and praying for those threatened by sea level rise. On the island of Samoa, during an international gathering of leaders of small island states, a high-ranking United Nations official waded out into the ocean with Samoan religious leaders and representatives of the World Council of Churches, attracting media attention for this unorthodox expression of concern.

The next day of prayer and action took place on September 21, 2014—the same day as the People's Climate March in New York City. OurVoices.net invited people around the world to join the Global Climate Chorus by going outside to pray for a climate agreement at one o'clock in the afternoon in their own time zone. Over nineteen thousand people responded from the US, the UK, Canada, Nigeria, Spain, Australia, New Zealand, India, and more. Churches that participated rang their bells. Rabbis sounded their shofars. Choirs went outside to sing. Others simply prayed silently. The Chorus attracted significant local media attention and gained OurVoices. net coverage in leading news services in several countries.

In December 2014, while government leaders were meeting for climate treaty negotiations in Lima, Peru, OurVoices.net organized #LightForLima, an effort designed to organize a series of vigils around the world, lit by solar lamps in place of the traditional candles. #LightForLima included vigils in major cities in the United States, United Kingdom, India, Australia, Europe, and hundreds of vigils in diverse local faith communities. A media campaign accompanied #LightForLima, raising awareness that large numbers of people of faith support the climate negotiations. OurVoices.net is one of the first international, multifaith environmental campaigns. Over thirty thousand people signed the OurVoices.net online call-to-action within the campaign's first three months, which bodes well for its long-term success.

Faith in Action

There are many ways that faith communities are taking action to protect the environment. Some are praying and educating. Others are reducing, reusing, and recycling. Others are advocating, bearing a cultural-political witness. Momentum is building, representing, in the words of author Paul Hawken, a "blessed unrest."

The environmental crisis is just that—a crisis. It also represents an opportunity for faith communities to evolve, to mobilize our ancient traditions to respond to new challenges in a new way. Some faith communities are making a comprehensive commitment to the environment through GreenFaith's Certification Program, a holistic, two-year process through which congregations integrate environmental themes into their worship, religious education, and spiritual practices; seven areas of their facility management; and their social outreach and public witness.[43] Faith communities in over thirty states have taken part, to spectacular effect. They've reduced their greenhouse gas emissions, the amount of waste they produce, and the amount of water they use. They've held compelling, energizing worship services that have moved and inspired their members. They've advocated for protections from pollution for some of the world's poorest communities. They've carried out interfaith environmental activities, bringing communities together that are, in other areas of life, at painful odds. And through these efforts, they've attracted new members and gained new relevance in their communities. While it is described as an environmental leadership program, the Certification Program truly is a growth and development initiative for faith communities.

At the turn of the new millenium, the environment was still an afterthought for most faith communities, a marginal topic that attracted little attention. But times have changed. The environment is now firmly planted on the radar screens of faith communities. Those communities will, without doubt, pay more and more attention to the fate of the earth, and what they can do to help heal God's creation.

Discussion Questions

1. The chapter describes many different kinds of environmental activities that faith communities are carrying out. Which of these would be a good fit for your faith community? Which would be the most challenging? Why? Do you sense God's call to your community in relation to any of these activities?

2. For some faith communities, addressing issues of legislative advocacy and environmental justice will be a harder challenge than offering prayers or educational programs on the environment, or making modifications in their consumption habits. Why is this the case? What role do you think faith communities should play in addressing major social concerns?

Chapter 8

Our Kairos Moment

Why Faith Must Become GreenFaith

In August of 2002, representatives of the nations of the world gathered in Johannesburg, South Africa, for the United Nations Summit on Sustainable Development. Thousands of people from around the globe assembled, people from diverse cultures and varying areas of expertise, creating an enthralling global mosaic. I had the good fortune to participate; it was the first such large-scale international meeting I'd ever attended. It was a remarkable experience, an awakening to the incredible diversity that constitutes the human family.

The Summit had two interrelated goals. First, those present sought to identify how the world's leaders could promote economic growth to lift to a better life the two billion people on the planet who live in dire poverty. Second, these same leaders aimed to identify how such dire poverty could be eliminated while at the same time restoring the environment, on which all our lives and all our economies depend.

The significance of these issues couldn't have been clearer. From the suffering and lost human potential that poverty inflicts to the illness and death that results from earth's degradation, the challenges we face came into startling focus. At the same time, the genuinely remarkable opportunity to create a world where a healthy environment creates a foundation for greater human well-being became equally vivid. And, the reality that time was running out was unavoidably clear. We simply can't keep degrading the environment without guaranteeing the breakdown of civilization in many parts of the world. It was impossible to remain detached.

The Summit resulted in no major diplomatic breakthroughs. But the gathering struck a profound chord, and it changed my life. To be together with so many gifted leaders for whom ending dire poverty and healing the earth represented top priorities—leaders from business, government, science, health care, labor, education, women's groups, youth, indigenous peoples, and faith—was a galvanizing conversion experience. All of a sudden, I saw that these two challenges are the defining issues of our time.

To call these two challenges "moral" or "spiritual" or "economic" or "political" shortchanges their significance. They are all of the above, and then more. Because of their magnitude, if we do not find a good solution to both extreme poverty and environmental degradation, our future is bleak. If we do not rise to these defining challenges, with all our human intelligence and power and wealth, it will represent not only a horrific infliction of suffering on billions of people, but also a truly tragic failure. Succeeding in our efforts to address these two challenges offers us an incredible opportunity to serve God, our Creator, the one who gives and sustains life. These goals can be met. It can be done. To miss this chance would not only be horribly sad. With all the gifts, skills, and assets that we have, it would be cruelly wrong.

Our Kairos Moment

Some Christian readers may be familiar with the Greek word *kairos,* which means "opportune moment, decisive time, fullness of time, supreme moment." The Ancient Greeks used two words to talk about time. One of these words, *chronos,* referred to normal, everyday time, the kind of time we experience from one moment to the next. *Kairos* was the second word the Ancient Greeks used for time. It described those particular times that arise only several times in a person's lifetime, times of great significance in which the decision that is made, the action taken, influences *everything* that follows. Originally used as a term from archery, *kairos* describes a fleeting moment during which an arrow must be fired precisely in order to hit a moving target, "a passing instant when an opening appears which must be driven through with force if success is to be achieved."[1]

In regards to the environment, we have reached our *kairos* moment. To protect and preserve life, we need forceful, decisive action. To create a healthy, prosperous future, we need change on a large scale. If we do not act now, all the evidence we have shows that the natural systems that support our lives will disintegrate, causing great harm and painful suffering. We must act, now.

Call to Action

The time has come for people of faith to make a commitment, a commitment to a future with clean air and water, productive lands, healthy rivers and oceans, an abundance of life, and a restored climate—and to an economy that creates good jobs that increase human and environmental well-being on a massive scale. This is a big, bold vision, commensurate with the challenges and dangers that we face. It's a solution that matches the scale of the problems we face—of dire poverty and environmental decline.

To achieve this future, society needs three things. Faith communities can help make each of these happen.

First, we need vision. We need a compelling vision of a future in which people and the planet thrive, to the mutual benefit of each. And with this vision, we need belief, the spiritual and moral energy that empowers us with the hope and confidence that this is possible. Faith communities are uniquely positioned to offer this vision.

Second, we need actual work—jobs and an economy that rewards actions that lift people out of poverty and restore the Earth at the same time. This work must change the course of our economy away from one that degrades and destroys Earth's life-giving capacity to one that restores and sustains it, while providing people around the globe with a dignified living. Members of faith communities can help make this economic transformation happen—with the assets that our communities control, and through the leadership of our members who run businesses, hold positions in government, and work within the nonprofit or educational sectors.

Finally, we need a new movement, an energized, relentless combination of commitment and community that can proclaim this vision and create this new reality. Religions, which have been movement incubators for millennia, are vital to this.

Let me be clear that religions alone cannot make this happen. We need partners in finance and government, in business and in healthcare and education and more. These partners, increasingly, have emerged. This transition is underway. But it needs to be accelerated, dramatically, because it is clear that we are running out of time. We don't have fifty years to commit to this transition. We don't even have a decade. We need to commit, and to act now. We need faiths to step forward, to use our collective influence in the service of this profoundly good, loving vision—eliminating dire poverty and restoring the earth.

Vision. Work. A movement. That is our new job, our top priority.

The Vision Thing

For many years, I attended a church with a beautiful stone pulpit. The solidness of the rock symbolized the unshakeable promise of God. The skillful carvings evoked an appreciation of beauty. The pulpit exemplified how architecture could elevate the senses, lift the soul to higher ground.

Bu there was one problem.

Carved across the top of the pulpit, engraved in stone, was a verse from the Bible: "Where there is no vision, the people perish" (Prov 29:18 KJV).

The first half of the verse ("Where there is no vision") was clearly visible throughout the church. Everyone could see it, no matter where they sat. But the second half ("the people perish") was hidden on the side of the pulpit, out of plain sight of most people in the church.

This made it seem as if the pulpit had an unfortunate name: "Where there is no vision."

Sadly, this first half of the Bible verse captures the incompleteness of most faith communities' understanding of the interconnectedness of human and ecological well-being. Too often, these concerns are seen as unrelated, or even in tension with each other, competing for attention and resources. A Catholic nun told me recently that several of her fellow sisters had told her that their work with poor communities was fundamentally different from her work to protect creation. "We care about people," they'd said, with the clear implication that protecting the environment had nothing to do with people. For many other faith communities, restoring the environment and a revitalized economy don't rate as priorities—the focus is more on individual salvation or responding to symptoms of problems rather than seeking systemic change. But the privatization of religion, in which the focus is solely on one's own spiritual well-being, is a dangerous trend that diminishes religion's dignity. And while responding to emergency needs with food and shelter is an important function of faith communities, it's long been known that charity alone does not equal true religion. We need systemic change, a new social-ecological compact.

It's no longer acceptable for faith communities to view poverty and the environment, the well-being of people and the well-being of the planet, in isolation from each other. The time has come. We need to green our faiths.

Higher Ground, Basic Needs

Today, faith communities need to set our eyes on higher ground. We need a vision that lifts up human and ecological flourishing as an undivided unity and our greatest moral priority. This vision must assert confidently that if we are serious about serving God, we must express this by seeking to eradicate extreme poverty and to heal the earth, with the recognition that *we simply cannot achieve one of these goals without achieving the other.*

We must express this vision in relationship to the most basic human needs, by recognizing that among these needs are our needs for health, for work, and for beauty. A commitment to restoring the earth and eliminating dire poverty can allow us to meet all three of these most fundamental human needs.

This vision is powerful because it addresses deep, real needs in a way that few other visions can. We need health. We need work. And we need beauty. None of these are optional. All of them are vital needs—not mere wants. When people are healthy, when they have good work, when they are exposed to beauty, they flourish. Conversely, a life without a good measure of all three of these things leaves human life impoverished, diminished, destroyed.

This isn't to say that protecting the environment represents the full solution to poverty or that eliminating poverty alone will restore the earth. Obviously, these challenges are more complex; education and healthcare, and other factors, are vitally important. But health, work, and beauty are fundamental. And, they are connected. By committing to a clean environment and an economy that puts people to work restoring the planet, we will literally generate human health. We will create millions, tens of millions of jobs that can lift people from poverty. We will heal the earth, making its beauty available to more and more people once again. Together, these themes represent a compelling vision that can galvanize faith communities, reenergizing ancient forms of religion and spirituality for a new day.

Healing People and the Planet

To rise from poverty, people need to be healthy; and to be healthy they need a clean environment. As we've learned, dirty air and polluted water, unhealthy food and toxic soil are no way to build a flourishing community. A recent, widely reported study found that people living in northern China have had their lives shortened, on average, five and a half years by air pollution.[2] Most of this pollution resulted from the burning of coal for heating, which forces people to breathe acrid, smoky air that leads to respiratory and cardiovascular disease on a massive scale. Over a three-decade period it will cause half a billion people to lose an aggregate two and a half billion years of life—due to air pollution. This is a staggering loss of life. And imagine the number of families thrown deeper into poverty by the premature loss of so many millions of people.

But it's not just the Chinese whose health suffers from dirty air or other forms of pollution. The World Health Organization reported that in 2012, over seven million people globally died from air pollution, an inconceivable level of loss.[3] And at any given time, the WHO reports also that nearly half the population of the developing world will be affected by an illness or disease directly linked to unsafe or too little water, poor or no sanitation, or faulty management of water resources.[4]

Think of these impacts, the impact that pollution has. Think of the loss of life, the number of children orphaned, the lost time with family and friends, the lost potential and productivity, the lost opportunities. How horribly, horribly tragic. Pollution degrades and destroys life. About this, faith communities must harbor no doubt.

Conversely, health researchers can also quantify the health benefits of various forms of environmental protection. As mentioned previously, the US Clean Air Act saves hundreds of thousands of lives every year, and saves millions of people from hospitalization and emergency room visits—simply by providing cleaner air. Reducing various forms of water pollution has similarly beneficial effects, preventing disease and supporting healthy communities by ensuring that people have clean water to drink.

Pollution Puts Poverty on Steroids

The issues of health, poverty, and pollution are impossible to separate. In addition to increasing illness and disease, a degraded environment is one of the most massive accelerators of poverty that exists. Droughts, one of climate change's direct impacts, devastate entire regions and turn subsistence farmers who were barely getting by into climate refugees who become homeless and have nowhere to live but refugee camps. The UN Environment Program projects that by 2050, there will be between three and four hundred million environmental refugees, people who have become homeless because climate change and other environmental threats have made forced them away from their homes. And, matters are getting worse. Many experts who have spent their lives seeking to reduce poverty in the developing world, and who have seen good results from their efforts, are now warning that all the progress of the past fifty years will be eradicated by climate change. The head of the World Bank, Jim Yong Kim, recently remarked that unchecked climate change will "trap millions of people in poverty."[5] He continued to say that climate change will "cause widespread food shortages, unprecedented heat-waves, and more intense cyclones... [and] could batter the slums even more and greatly harm the lives and the hopes of individuals and families who have had little hand in raising the Earth's temperature."[6]

Not exactly a prescription for poverty alleviation.

Faith communities need to be clear that they stand on the side of health and well-being, for people and the planet. The evidence is overwhelmingly clear that this is consistent with the deepest values and commitments of our churches and synagogues, our mosques and temples. Why would we not take the strongest of stands?

Get to Work

We've seen that pollution sickens billions of people and worsens poverty—and that a healthier environment makes for healthier people. We must now address the fact that restoring the earth is a massive job, one that can't be carried out by volunteer efforts and goodwill alone. Similarly, solving dire poverty requires opportunities for work on an equally massive scale. Faith communities need to proclaim a bold vision that prioritizes and connects these two vital goals.

The need for a decent, dignified job is one of our most basic needs. The availability of good work makes everything else possible. Work provides both income and, in many cases, a sense of purpose. It is a foundation for family life, the support of children, and the well-being of a community. It can elevate the poor and create opportunity where none previously existed. Without work, people are impoverished and their lives dissipated. Despite the Bible's suggestion that God created work to punish Adam and Eve after kicking them out of the garden, there are few things more important than a good, even meaningful, job. A safe, secure job and a healthy working environment are top priorities for most adults—and always will be. Almost nothing is more important.

The Great Recession of 2009 has created deep levels of concern that the long-term job prospects in the US are poor. The unemployment rate, while it has decreased in the past few years, still remains too high, with the ranks of the permanently unemployed or underemployed exacerbating the high levels of income inequality that has everyone worried. And, suffering from unemployment is a global phenomenon. The International Labor Organization reports that 1.3 billion workers and their dependents struggle to survive on less than $2 daily, the threshold economists use to measure dire poverty.[7] It is impossible to overstate the importance of creating jobs, good jobs.

Jobs and the Environment—Partners in Prosperity

Over the past decade, a revolution in thinking about the link between the environment and the economy has taken place. The relationship between these two used to be understood as a negative one—that protecting the environment represented a drag on the economy. An image in an earlier chapter captured this negative correlation by describing a photo of farmers protesting a proposal to limit water withdrawals from a river for irrigation in order to protect an endangered fish. The photo showed a protesting farmer holding up a sign that reads, "People are more important than fish."

Tensions between certain forms of economic activity and the environment do exist. But the tired, false, self-defeating orthodoxy that pits economic well-being irrevocably against a healthy, sustainable environment is giving way to a dynamic, hopeful, new reality—that "protecting the environment—in particular, defeating global warming—can also be an effective engine of economic growth, job creation, and even poverty reduction."[8]

What's a Green Job?

In the early 2000s, the US Bureau of Labor Statistics (BLS) began to measure the number of "green jobs" in the United States, just as it had measured the number of jobs in other sectors of the economy for decades. According to their definition, green jobs include jobs focused on generating energy from renewable sources, increasing energy efficiency, pollution reduction and removal, natural resource conservation, environmental compliance, training, and public awareness. Green jobs make "their establishment's production processes more environmentally friendly or use fewer natural resources. These workers research, develop, or use technologies and practices to lessen the environmental impact of their establishment, or train the establishment's workers or contractors in these technologies and practices.[9]

In 2012, the BLS reported that there were 3.1 million green jobs in the United States. At the same time, the fossil fuel industry employed approximately 3.5 million people.[10] These numbers show that the green jobs category, a relative newcomer on the employment scene, is no bit player.

It's not just the number of green jobs that's impressive; it's the fact that they pay well, also. The same 2012 BLS report noted that green jobs paid, on average, $7,000 more annually than the average job created across the rest of the economy.[11] Green-job growth is spread across the country, with states in the Southeast and Midwest seeing particularly strong growth and the construction and manufacturing industries benefitting substantially. These are jobs that sustain families and communities and pay a decent wage while helping protect and restore the earth, a genuinely winning formula.

Let's look deeper into one particular sector of the green economy—the solar industry. This industry now supports over 140,000 jobs nationwide, and the rate of solar job growth has been ten times the rate of job growth across the economy.[12] Solar installer jobs, one of the fastest-growing subcategories within this sector, pay between $20 to $25 per hour and represent the kinds of skilled trade jobs that our economy desperately needs.[13] Some skeptics might wonder if this is all the result of excessive government subsidies—but that is not the case. Rather, traditional economies of scale are starting to take effect. The cost of solar panels has dropped 80 percent since 2007. Government incentives for solar have dropped 85 percent in the past decade. The industry is beginning to mature.[14]

The Answer Is Blowin' in the Wind

It's not just the solar industry—the wind sector has grown with similar speed. Wind power now supplies the electricity for fifteen million US homes. Double digit growth has become the norm for the wind industry over the past decade.[15] The only time period the industry's growth slowed was during the government slowdown known as "the sequestration" at the end of 2012, when the renewal of government tax policies was thrown into question. In other words, the industry was not the problem. A broken political process was.

Increasingly, studies have shown that investments in renewable energy yield far stronger returns in job creation than do similar investments in the fossil fuel industry. Robert Pollin has written that investments in renewable energy create "about seven-

152

teen jobs for every $1 million in outlays, whereas spending the same $1 million in the oil and coal industries creates about 5.5 jobs." In other words, he continues, "the job-creation effect of green investments is more than three times larger than that for fossil fuel production."[16] Imagine the potential benefits if the world's governments were to shift the $1.5 billion in subsidies that the fossil fuel industry receives *daily* into the renewable energy economy. The results would be staggeringly good—for the environment and for the tens of millions of jobs that would be created.

The renewable energy economy is just one sector of the larger green economy, an economy with incredible promise for creating good jobs that lift people from poverty while restoring creation. A commitment to this economy represents a deeply moral vision for our future—a future in which our economy creates good jobs that lift people from poverty, restores the environment, and creates a healthy environment for life. Faith communities must embrace this vision and advocate with urgency to see it made real.

Inevitably, over time, some industries will suffer job losses as the green economy picks up speed. Faith communities need to call for governmental and industry support for a "just transition," for retraining and other service to help people retool and get back to work. The United States lags far behind the rest of the world in regards to this kind of support, and it ends up costing us. It's far better to retrain displaced workers and to get them into a new career than it is to let them languish on the unemployment rolls. A 2012 study of developed countries showed that actively retraining workers reduced unemployment and increased GDP by more than the cost of the retraining programs, making this approach a true win-win.[17] Economic transitions, especially those on the scale that we are discussing here, inevitably result in some jobs disappearing as new ones come into being. This research shows that a solid investment in retraining is not only the right thing to do. It also results in a measurable net profit.

Oh, Beautiful...

The miracle is not to walk on water. The miracle is to walk on the green Earth in this present moment.[18]

—Thich Nhat Hanh

People need health. People need work. People also need beauty.

At first, some will react that beauty is nice, but that it is optional, a luxury. They are wrong. Beauty, in the form of exposure to the natural world, is vital to human well-being. Without a relationship to nature, our lives are gravely diminished, to the detriment of our families, ourselves, and society.

This isn't just sentimentality. It's well supported by numerous studies and reams of data. Consider some of these stories.

"Planting Justice"

California's San Quentin State Prison is not exactly the kind of place where one envisions nature's beauty as making a measurable difference in people's lives. But the nonprofit group Planting Justice, through its Insight Gardening Program, has launched a five-bed organic garden where inmates grow flowers and vegetables while developing skills that lead to better jobs after their release. This program is one of many around the country that seeks to reduce recidivism rates and prepare inmates for successful reentry into society. The medium for the program's success? Time spent outdoors, gardening.

Nationally, recidivism rates are approximately 40 percent, meaning that four out of every ten prison inmates end up back in jail. Planting Justice has cut that rate by 75 percent—only one in ten of their graduates returns to jail. In the bright sun, next to one of the raised gardening beds, one inmate named Charles speaks with infectious joy about the reward he feels from growing fresh tomatoes. His fellow inmate, George, adds, "This is a spiritual act also. It's called 'insight gardening'; we work on our own inner selves as well as on the garden."[19]

Projects such as these save state and local governments hundreds of thousands of dollars, and help heal people's lives. What's not to like?

Thinking Clearly

A second perspective on the vital importance to our lives of nature and its beauty comes from a different direction. Since 1999, numerous published studies show that students who are exposed to more natural light in the classroom learn more than students who worked under more artificial lighting. These studies demonstrate a "statistically compelling connection between day lighting and student performance."[20] Studies showed that students scored between 7 and 26 percent higher on standardized tests when exposed to more natural light, a stunning increase. Researchers expressed amazement at these findings, in part because the reigning assumption in the field of school design was that a view of the outdoors was to be avoided in classrooms—because it represented a distraction for students.[21] When we are exposed to nature's light, nature's beauty, we learn better. Measurably better.

But we don't just think better—we feel better too. Study after study has shown that "hospital patients who viewed natural scenes; for example, trees and animals from their wards, recovered faster, spent less time in hospital, required fewer painkillers, and had fewer postoperative complications than those patients whose ward views consisted of other buildings and which were devoid of any appearance of plants and animals."[22] Workers with views of nature are more productive than those whose offices look only onto other buildings or roads. Drivers on roads where there are trees planted along the roadside are calmer and have lower blood pressure than drivers along roads devoid of trees. Prisoners with views of nature out their cell windows make fewer visits to the infirmary than those who only see concrete. Recent immigrants' stress levels are measurably lowered if they have regular contact with nature. And, to cap it off, there's an overwhelming body of evidence about the health benefits of regular contact with animals.[23] No rational person can doubt the utility of nature's beauty when faced with this body of evidence.

In life, every person needs to learn. Every person needs to heal. We all have these needs; they are ubiquitous, unavoidable. Done poorly, they are also costly. For our society and government, education and healthcare represent two of our largest expenses. By learning how to reconnect our educational and health systems with nature, by reconnecting nature with learning and with healing, we can enrich our society in vital and valuable ways. Calling this a luxury is shortsighted and inhumane. Given the enormous body of evidence, it is also an expensive mistake that we can't afford.

Becoming Wise

Allow me to return one final time to the theme on which this book began—the value of spiritual experience outdoors. I won't rehash the case I made for the importance of these experiences in our growth and development as people. But I do want to reemphasize that fact that a strong relationship with the natural world helps us be spiritually alive and wise.

We've explored at length the idea that contact with nature restores and enlivens our souls. Such contact is not a luxury good, or an *environmental amenity,* a term that environmental economists are fond of. The experience of nature's beauty enhances our ability to learn. It makes us more resilient, more able to heal from life's inevitable challenges and injuries, whether physical or emotional. Along with our health and a decent job, access to nature's beauty is among our basic needs. It should not be optional any more than food or a decent job should be optional.

The End of the World as We Know It

We've seen a vision of human-environmental healing, well-being, and wisdom. We've seen that a green revolution is already underway. Faith communities now have a choice to make. They can cling to the past, ignoring the fundamental challenge and opportunity of our time. Or they can rise to the occasion on behalf of our shared future.

I recently visited Germany for a series of environmental meetings with a group of religious leaders, organized by the World Council of Churches. We spent several days in the Rhineland, in Germany's northwestern corner. This has long been Germany's energy region, with coal mines traditionally supplying much of the country's electric power. Within the course of a single day, we saw an old world passing away and a new one coming into being.

As we drove through the fields of the countryside, several large smokestacks and cooling towers rose up above the horizon. As we got closer, we saw a large coal plant, with a waste incinerator located right next to it. The plant was enormous. The smoke poured out of its chimneys and cooling towers like the churning, angry whitewater of a mighty river.

We drove past the plant, and approached a low ridge. When we crested the ridge, a gaping hole in the earth, several miles wide and over a thousand feet deep, opened up before us. It was the largest open pit coal mine in the country, the source of the coal that the nearby plant was burning.

After touring the edge of the mine, we met in a church in the town closest to the mine. The congregation had previously worshiped in a village that no longer existed—because it had been bulldozed so that the mine could be expanded. The entire village—church, hundreds of homes, stores, and all—had been relocated and rebuilt, from scratch. Even the small river that flowed through the previous town had been rerouted away from the mine. "It was sad," said one of the leaders of our group who had observed the relocation process. "People who had lived in that town for years were simply forced to move. All their memories, all their familiar places were gone." The mine is scheduled to be closed in 2020 as part of Germany's *energiewende,* or "energy transformation," the most aggressive governmental clean energy policy in the developed world.

For a short time, we spoke with the church's pastor, an energetic, healthy young man who clearly cared deeply for the people of his congregation. The pastor had a background as an environmental activist, which made his placement in this particular community surprising. When asked if the air quality in the community suffered from closeness to the coal plant, he answered, "Do you want the official story or what is really happening?" When we said we wanted both, he told us that company officials claimed that there were no health impacts from the plant's operation. "But my two boys have asthma," he said, "and a lot of other people in the community do also." The coal mine and the church were located in a rural area, miles from any urban center. It was difficult to envision other sources of air pollution leading to high asthma levels.

Others in our group asked how many in his congregation worked at the coal mine or plant. "A lot of them do," he said. "They're glad to have a decent-paying job, and I can understand that ultimately it's not my role here to be critical of their work. The mine and the plant are already scheduled to close; nothing I do will accelerate or change that. The coal company has simply stopped hiring new people; they are slowly and surely reducing their workforce by attrition." There was a sense of loss over the entire scene, as if a tragic chapter of a long story was coming to an end. The pastor's stoic directness was refreshingly honest, if sad.

Ten miles away, we visited a small neighborhood church in the town of Heimsburg. The church had been built in the 1960s, and needed a renovation early in the 2010s. The church's leaders believed that caring for creation and addressing climate change were central to their identity, so when they began planning for their renovation, one of their main goals was to make the church an environmental model. They hired an architect who had created the "passive house" system, a building design process that cut the energy use of the average building 80 percent below the already stringent German building code requirements. The new building's windows were triple glazed and the insulation incredibly tight, making the facility almost leak-free. At the same time, to ensure an adequate supply of fresh air, a set of highly efficient air pumps circulated fresh air throughout the facility. During our two-hour meeting with nearly forty people in a fairly small room, the air never once seemed stale, and no one was yawning.

Furthermore, no energy was used to heat the building while we were visiting. As the architect explained, "Each of your bodies produces one hundred watts of heat on an ongoing basis. The system circulates that heat and no fuel is burned." The electricity for the church lighting is generated by a solar array on the church roof. On an annual basis, the church generates more power than it uses, and sells the power back to the grid. "We were able to train a number of new workers as we carried out this project," the architect said. "They have new skills which they can take to new jobs." The day following our meeting, the architect was travelling to China to launch a "passive building" project there.

In addition to its remarkable energy systems, the renovation was beautiful. A clear window behind the altar looked out onto a small reflecting pool fed by a simple metal fountain. Past the fountain, a stained glass window from the original church stood, illuminated by daylight. Back inside, in the basement of the church, was a stunning, silent chapel, minimalist in style with concrete walls and a skylight allowing natural light to shine onto a simple cross and rack of candles. It was a genuinely holy place.

After visiting the Heimsburg church, we met with officials at the regional church office, where the officials described the training that they carried out with more than one hundred congregations in their region, seeking to integrate energy efficiency, conservation, and renewable energy into the operations of all their congregations. "We are proud of our country's *energiewende* and we want it to succeed," said one of the regional church leaders. "God made this beautiful Earth, and we must protect it. The faith community must be a leader." At the entrance to the regional offices was a meter that displayed the energy produced by the solar array on the office roof. Along with the energy, the number of tons of carbon dioxide emissions prevented was also shown.

At the end of the day, the tragic dimension resurfaced. A member of our delegation, a Welsh woman who lives in Fiji, spoke about her work with the Pacific Conference of Churches, helping the Fijian government develop policies and plans to manage the relocation of Fijians who need to move because of rising sea levels. "We had our first three villages that needed to move last year," she said. "It's incredibly hard work. It's very emotionally painful for the people who have to move, and it's bloody hard to find new places for them to live. It's not as if there's a lot of free land just sitting around, our countries saying, 'Hey—why don't you just come settle here?'" She estimated that across the Pacific Islands, more than half a million people would eventually be forced to move, a small fraction of the fifty to two hundred million worldwide who will need to do so by 2050.[24] "For people whose countries go underwater, we have no official way of defining their status," she said. "If there country is underground, where is their citizenship? Where is home?"

Our Green Transformation

Germany has its *energiewende,* its energy transformation. But this isn't a book about someone else's transformation, or some other country's. It's a book about yours, and about ours.

So now, it is time for you to decide. Do you believe that God calls us to care for creation? Do you believe, as a matter of your faith, that you are called to respond? If your answer is yes, what will you do?

I've outlined three ways in which we're called to respond—by deepening our relationship with God and God's good earth, by changing our consumption habits to protect creation, and by advocating for policies that will create an environmentally healthy future. What will you do in relation to each of these?

How will you strengthen your relationship with the natural world? How will you cultivate a greater reverence for the earth, for the animals and plants, the air, soil, and water that sustain your life? Will you spend more time outdoors—in relaxation and in contemplation? Will you read the sacred texts of your tradition with an eye for the many ways that God's creation is valued? Will you pray not only for the people you love but also for the natural world?

How will you change your consumption habits, the ways in which you use natural resources? Will you reduce your use of energy and water? Will you reset your thermostats to be just a bit cooler in winter and warmer in summer? Will you eat less meat, understanding its large ecological cost? Will you make sure that the next car you buy is a high-mileage vehicle, that the next furnace in your home is as efficient as possible?

How will you work to create a more environmentally sustainable and just society? Will you contact your elected officials, urging them to support stronger environmental policies? Would you be willing to meet with these officials in person to voice your views, to attend a demonstration to express your grave concern, to take part in a community organizing effort to marshal the influence to force change?

How will you live differently? The question is a vital one. You must not duck it.

GreenFaith exists to help you answer these questions. We can provide you with prayers and spiritual tools to help you connect with God outdoors. Through our GreenFaith Day Program, we provide resources to help faith communities select a single day when they offer one prayer and take one simple action to protect the planet. Through our GreenFaith Shield Program, an environmental merit badge initiative, your faith community can take action over a month—spiritual and practical, at your faith community and at the homes of your members—to earn the GreenFaith Shield and make a measurable difference for the planet. If your faith community wants to make a major commitment, you can enroll in our Certification Program, the transformative two-year process that I described above. Or perhaps you yourself feel drawn to religiously based environmental leadership—in which case the GreenFaith Fellowship Program, an interfaith environmental leadership training program, may be for you. No organization offers a more comprehensive set of programs and resources to empower you, and your faith community, to engage these vital concerns. You can learn more at www.greenfaith.org, or by contacting me at revfharper@greenfaith.org.

Are you ready to join with others to make a difference—one that will have lasting impact?

This list of questions, and of options, may seem overwhelming. Start small and simple. Now—right now—begin by taking a walk outside to commune with God. Listen to God's voice. Meditate on God's ways. You are a caretaker of God's earth. Ask God how you can take your role more seriously.

Coming Home

This question—where is home?— is the defining question of our time.

The first answer to this question is simple and clear. Our home is the earth, a single, stunningly beautiful planet that supports life in a way that no other place we know does or can. We have no other home, no other source of air, of water, of food, of life. For reasons we cannot fathom, God has made it possible for us to love and to work, to suffer and to enjoy, to live and to die—on earth. Life on earth is a remarkable privilege, a remarkable gift.

Now, we must make our appreciation of that gift concretely real. We have been given a gift. We must reciprocate. We have been loved. We must love in return. We must step out in faith and act.

As we've seen throughout this book, environmental trends are not good. This is not meant to overwhelm you, but to motivate you with the truth. All of earth's eco-systems, which provide air and water, food and habitation, are in decline. It is painful and hard to say so, but we must. It is unavoidable and inevitable. It may be a hard truth, but burying our heads in the sand will ensure large-scale destruction. Change is up to you. It's up to us. Together we can make needed changes. We've done it before. For the sake of our children and theirs, we must do it again.

In our ingenuity and creativity, we have discovered many of the technologies that can reverse those trends. More and more, we have the means of creating a pathway to a loving, shared future in which life abounds. But this path will not choose us. We must embrace it, with all our moral and intellectual and financial and creative might.

At times, this will be inconvenient. At times, it will feel overwhelming. At times, this shift will force us to give up old, comfortable ways and step forward into an unfamiliar future. At times, we may suffer. But step forward we must—or life will, in many ways and on a dreadfully large scale, die.

We must choose life. We must choose now.

To be a person of faith, a spiritual person, now means to love the earth as well as loving people. For faith communities, the environment must now be front and center on the agenda. There is no other way. These concerns will affect us all. We must pray and learn, act and advocate, for a godly relationship with the earth.

Each generation faces an overarching challenge, the one in relation to which we are judged. This is ours.

Will your faith become green faith?

Discussion Questions

1. This chapter begins by offering a vision of protecting the planet and reducing dire poverty. What are your reactions to this vision and to the way it is presented?

2. This chapter mixes religion with politics—and with public issues. How do you react to this? Do you agree that people of faith, and faith communities, should work not only to help people transform their private lives but also society as a whole?

3. The chapter concludes by inviting you to make a choice—and to take concrete steps to connect with God outdoors, to change your consumption habits, and to advocate for an environmentally sustainable, just future. Can you think of one specific thing that you can do in each of these areas in the coming month? Share these ideas with others in your group. Which are easiest and which are hard? Why?

Notes

1. Raw Awe

1. This well-known hymn represents an expression of awe and joy at the majesty of creation. After describing the stunning beauty of the earth, the refrain of the hymn reads as follows: "Then sings my soul, my Savior God, to thee: How great thou art! How great thou art!"

2. Job 42:3.

3. Rudolf Otto, *The Idea of the Holy*, trans. John W. Harvey (London: Oxford University Press, 1923), https://archive.org/details/theideaoftheholy00ottouoft.

4. James M. Gustafson, *Ethics from a Theocentric Perspective*, vol. 1 (Chicago: University of Chicago Press, 1981), 209; and Gene Marshall, *The Call of the Awe: Rediscovering Christian Profundity in an Irreligious Era* (Lincoln, NE: Writers Club Press, 2002).

5. Qur'an 42:29, Ali Quli Qara'i, *The Qur'an: With a Phrase-by-Phrase English Translation* (London: ICAS Press, 2004), http://al-quran.info/#42:29.

6. "Francis Bacon > Quotes > Quotable Quote," Goodreads, http://www.goodreads.com/quotes/66310-god-has-in-fact-written-two-books-not-just-one. Many conservative Christians are very comfortable with this understanding of the natural world. For example, Bacon's conclusion cited here is also noted on the website of Creation Ministries international, a leading proponent of creationism. See http://creation.com/sir-francis-bacon.

2. Good, Good, and Very Good

1. Sharon Basaraba, "Longevity Throughout History: How has human life expectancy changed over time?," About Health, May 11, 2013, http://longevity.about.com/od/longevitystatsandnumbers/a/Longevity-Throughout-History.htm.

2. Ramban (Nachmanides), *Commentary on the Torah: Deuteronomy*, translated and annotated with index by Rabbi Dr. Charles B. Chavel (New York: Shilo Publishing, Inc., 1976), 265.

3. For the commandment, see Deut 6:5, 13. For Rabbi Troster's excellent article, "Ten Jewish Teachings on the Environment," http://greenfaith.org/religious-teachings/jewish-statements-on-the-environment/ten-jewish-teachings-on-judaism-and-the-environment/ten-jewish-teachings-on-judaism-and-the-environment/.

4. *Mishneh Torah, Sepher Madah, Hilkhot Yesodei Ha-Torah* 2:1-2.

5. Ps 111:10.

6. For example, see Yonatan Neril, "Judaism and Environmentalism: Bal Tashchit," Chabad, footnote 2, accessed November 29, 2013, http://www.chabad.org/library/article_cdo/aid/1892179/jewish/Judaism-and-Environmentalism-Bal-Tashchithtm#footnote2a1892179.

7. Yonatan Neril, "Judaism and Environmentalism: Bal Tashchit," Chabad, http://www.chabad.org/library/article_cdo/aid/1892179/jewish/Judaism-and-Environmentalism-Bal-Tashchit.htm

8. Ibid.

9. *Midrash Kohelet Rabbah*, 1 on Ecclesiastes 7:13.

3. For the Bible Tells Me So

1. For the source of this comment, and an engaging response, see the response of the Reverend Dr. Russ Pierson and Dr. John Roe, "Does God Love the World?" *Huffington Post*, last updated July 8, 2013, http://www.huffingtonpost.com/russ-pierson/does-god-love-the-world_b_3239756.html.

2. Dan Neary, "Not Just Wheat and Grapes," *Work and Calling* (blog), August 5, 2013, http://www.workandcalling.com/2013/08/not-just-wheat-and-grapes.html.

4. Many Faiths, One Earth

1. These figures are taken from the Pew Research Center's Forum on Religion and Public Life's "Global Religious Landscape" Study published in December 2012, which can be found at http://www.pewforum.org/2012/12/18/global-religious-landscape-exec/.

2. Huston Smith, *The World's Religions* (San Francisco: HarperSanFrancisco, 1991).

3. For Grim's important definition of indigenous lifeways, see "Indigenous Traditions and Ecology," The Forum on Religion and Ecology at Yale (1998), http://fore.research.yale.edu /religion/indigenous/.

4. John Grim, "Recovering Religious Ecology with Indigenous Traditions," The Forum on Religion and Ecology at Yale, http://fore.research.yale.edu/files/Grim_Recovering_Reli gious_Ecology_with_Indigenous_Traditions.pdf.

5. James Howard Kunstler, *The Geography of Nowhere: The Rise and Decline of America's Man-Made Landscape* (New York: Touchstone, 1994).

6. "Indigenous People," Food and Agriculture Organization of the United Nations, accessed August 26, 2012, http://www.fao.org/biodiversity/cross-sectoral-issues/indigenous -people/en/.

7. Claudia Sobrevilla, "The Role of Indigenous Peoples in Biodiversity Conservation: The Natural but Often Forgotten Partners," The World Bank (May 2008), accessed August 26, 2012, http://siteresources.worldbank.org/INTBIODIVERSITY/Resources/RoleofIndig enousPeoplesinBiodiversityConservation.pdf.

8. *Gary Nabhan* (blog), http://garynabhan.com/.

9. See, for example, Veda Kalpataru, an online Hindu resource center, http://vedakalpa taru.com/?page_id=172.

10. "Hindu Statements on the Environment," GreenFaith, http://greenfaith.org/reli gious-teachings/hindu-statements-on-the-environment.

11. Ibid.

12. For this, and other useful facts about the impact of household consumption, see "Ten Personal Solutions to Global Warming," Union of Concerned Scientists, last revised October 17, 2013, http://www.ucsusa.org/global_warming/what_you_can_do/ten-personal-solutions -to.html.

13. See the list of all 177 countries at "Meat Consumption per Person," Scribd, http:// www.scribd.com/doc/91840616/Meat-Consumption-Per-Person.

14. Maurice R Landes, "The Elephant Is Jogging," *Amber Waves* vol. 2, issue. 1 (February 2004), http://ageconsearch.umn.edu/bitstream/131785/2/features_elephant.pdf.

15. For a detailed examination of the history of the Bishnois and other examples of Hindu environmental teaching and practice, see Pankaj Jain, *Dharma and Ecology of Hindu Communities: Sustenance and Sustainability*, Ashgate New Critical Thinking in Religion, Theology, and Biblical Studies (Surrey, UK, and Burlington, VT: Ashgate, 2011).

16. "Chipko Movement," India International Institute for Sustainable Development, December 2007, http://www.iisd.org/50comm/commdb/desc/d07.htm.

17. For Dr. Stephanie Kaza's excellent overview of Buddhist teachings on the environment, see "Buddhist Teachings and the Environment," GreenFaith (March 19, 2012), http://greenfaith.org/files/buddhist-environmental-slides-stephanie-kaza.

18. Ibid.

19. Alan Watts "Transcending Duality 2 of 2," *Alan Watts Podcast* (blog), http://www.alanwattspodcast.com/index.php?post_id=373289.

20. Thich Nhat Hanh, "The First Precept: Reverence for Life," Buddhism in the National Capitol of Canada, http://dharma.ncf.ca/introduction/precepts/precept-1.html.

21. Stephanie Kaza, "Buddhist Teachings and the Environment," GreenFaith (March 19, 2012), http://greenfaith.org/files/buddhist-environmental-slides-stephanie-kaza.

22. Louise Story, "Anywhere the Eye Can See, It's Likely to See an Ad," *New York Times* online (January 15, 2007), http://www.nytimes.com/2007/01/15/business/media/15everywhere.html?pagewanted=all&_r=0.

23. For a detailed recounting of this story and the entire phenomenon of tree ordinations, see Susan M. Darlington, "The Ordination of a Tree: The Buddhist Ecology Movement in Thailand," *Ethnology*, vol. 37, no. 1 (Winter 1998), http://ccbs.ntu.edu.tw/FULLTEXT/JR-ADM/susan.htm.

24. Ibid.

25. James Miller, "Daoism and Ecology," The Forum on Religion and Ecology at Yale (1998), http://fore.research.yale.edu/religion/daoism/.

26. *Tao Te Ching*, chapter 16, http://acc6.its.brooklyn.cuny.edu/~phalsall/texts/taote-v1.txt.

27. Mary Evelyn Tucker, "Confucianism and Ecology: Potential and Limits," The Forum on Religion and Ecology at Yale (1998), http://fore.research.yale.edu/religion/confucianism/.

28. Ibid.

29. Sahih Bukhari, Volume 1, Book 1, Number 3, http://www.sahih-bukhari.com/Pages/Bukhari_1_01.php.

30. Islam has Five Pillars: Shahadah—declaring there is no god except God, and Muhammad is God's Messenger; Salat—prayer five times a day; Sawm—fasting and self-control

during the season of Ramadan; Zakat—giving to the poor; Hajj—making r
Mecca at least once in a lifetime, if one is able.

31. Qur'an 22:18, Ali Quli Qara'i, *The Qur'an: With a Phrase-by-Phrase English Transla-tion* (London: ICAS Press, 2004), http://al-quran.info/#22:18.

32. Ali Quli Qara'i, *The Qur'an: With a Phrase-by-Phrase English Translation* (London: ICAS Press, 2004), http://al-quran.info/#24:45.

33. Ali Quli Qara'i, *The Qur'an: With a Phrase-by-Phrase English Translation* (London: ICAS Press, 2004), http://al-quran.info/#6:38.

34. "The Experience and Doctrine of Love in Ibn 'Arabî," *The Muhyiddin Ibn 'Arabî Society* (2002), http://www.ibnarabisociety.org/articles/addas1.html.

35. Frederick Mathewson Denny, "The Meaning of 'Ummah' in the Qur'an," in *History of Religions* (Chicago: The University of Chicago Press, 1975) 15 (1): 34–70.

36. Ali Quli Qara'i, *The Qur'an: With a Phrase-by-Phrase English Translation* (London: ICAS Press, 2004), http://al-quran.info/#42:29.

37. Ibrahim Abdul-Matin, *Green Deen: What Islam Teaches about Protecting the Planet* (San Francisco: Berrett-Koehler, 2010) represents a useful introduction to the topic of Islamic teaching on the environment. Mr. Abdul-Matin included this comment in his book and also shared these comments during a lecture he presented for GreenFaith on January 6, 2011.

38. Augustine of Hippo, a great fifth-century Christian theologian, wrote: "Some people, in order to discover God, read books. But there is a great book: the very appearance of created things. Look above you! Look below you! Note it. Read it. God, whom you want to discover, never wrote that book with ink. Instead He set before your eyes the things that He had made. Can you ask for a louder voice than that? Why, heaven and earth shout to you: 'God made me!'" (De Civit. Dei, Book XVI).

39. Qur'an 33:72, Ali Quli Qara'i, *The Qur'an: With a Phrase-by-Phrase English Transla-tion* (London: ICAS Press, 2004), http://al-quran.info/#33:72.

40. Ibid.

41. Ibid.

42. Qur'an 25:43, Ali Quli Qara'i, *The Qur'an: With a Phrase-by-Phrase English Transla-tion* (London: ICAS Press, 2004), http://al-quran.info/#25:43.

43. Qur'an 7:31, Ali Quli Qara'i, *The Qur'an: With a Phrase-by-Phrase English Translation* (London: ICAS Press, 2004), http://al-quran.info/#7:31.

44. Ibrahim Abdul-Matin, *Green Deen: What Islam Teaches about Protecting the Planet* (San Francisco: Berrett-Koehler, 2010).

45. Qur'an 55:1-7, Ali Quli Qara'i, *The Qur'an: With a Phrase-by-Phrase English Translation* (London: ICAS Press, 2004), http://al-quran.info/#55.

46. Fazlun M Khalid, "Islam and the Environment," in *Encyclopedia of Global Environmental Change*, vol. 5, ed. Peter Timmerman (Chichester: John Wiley & Sons, 2002), 332–39.

5. What's in a Word?

1. Henry David Thoreau, *Walden*, "Quotes about Wilderness," Goodreads, http://www.goodreads.com/Quotes/tag/wilderness.

2. Intergovernmental Panel on Climate Change, *Climate Change 2013: The Physical Science Basis: Summary for Policymakers*, AR5, p. 3, http://einstitute.worldbank.org/ei/warmerworld/docs/warmerworld_pdfs_IPCC%20Fifth%20Assessment%20Report,%20Climate%20Change%202013.pdf.

3. Bjorn Lomborg, "Cool It," Bjorn Lomborg: Get the facts straight, http://lomborg.com/cool-it.

4. "The Clean Air Act and the Economy," United States Environmental Protection Agency, http://www.epa.gov/air/sect812/economy.html.

5. "Neat Facts about United States Agriculture," Farmers Edge (July 4, 2013), http://www.farmersedge.ca/blog/2013/07/04/neat-facts-about-united-states-agriculture.

6. "Employment by Major Industry Sector," Bureau of Labor Statistics (December 19, 2013), http://www.bls.gov/emp/ep_table_201.htm.

7. Jennifer Chu, "Air Pollution Causes 200,000 Early Deaths Each Year in the U.S.," Laboratory for Aviation and the Environment, Massachusetts Institute of Technology (August 29, 2013), http://lae.mit.edu/air-pollution-causes-200000-early-deaths-each-year-in-the-u-s/.

6. The Pale Blue Dot

1. Carl Sagan, *Pale Blue Dot* (New York: Ballantine Books, 1994), 6–7.

2. "Abraham Joshua Heschel > Quotes > Quotable Quotes," Goodreads, http://www.goodreads.com/quotes/51262-our-goal-should-be-to-live-life-in-radical-amazement.

3. "Ocean," *Wikipedia*, http://en.wikipedia.org/wiki/Ocean.

4. "Interesting Ocean Facts," Save the Sea, http://www.savethesea.org/STS%20ocean_facts.htm.

5. Kathy Svitil, "Survival beneath the Surface," Public Broadcasting Service, http://www.pbs.org/wnet/savageseas/deep-article.html.

6. "Interesting Ocean Facts," Save the Sea, http://www.savethesea.org/STS%20ocean_facts.htm.

7. "Frequently Asked Questions (FAQ)," Census of Marine Life (2010), http://www.coml.org/media-resources/frequently-asked-questions-faq.

8. The Ocean Portal Team, "The Census of Marine Life," Ocean Portal: Smithsonian National Museum of Natural Life, http://ocean.si.edu/census-marine-life.

9. Ibid.

10. Bob Drogin, "Mapping an Ocean of Species," *Los Angeles Times* online (August 2, 2009), http://articles.latimes.com/2009/aug/02/nation/na-fish2.

11. "Coral," National Geographic online, http://animals.nationalgeographic.com/animals/invertebrates/coral/.

12. Robert Roy Britt, "Mystery of Ocean Glow Confirmed in Satellite Photos," Live Science (October 4, 2005), http://www.livescience.com/9387-mystery-ocean-glow-confirmed-satellite-photos.html.

13. Bob Drogin, "Mapping an Ocean of Species," *Los Angeles Times* online (August 2, 2009), http://articles.latimes.com/2009/aug/02/nation/na-fish2/2.

14. David Braun, "Coral Reefs Provide Services Worth $172 Billion to Humans Every Year," *National Geographic* online (October 16, 2009), http://newswatch.nationalgeographic.com/2009/10/16/corals_provide_vast_human_services/.

15. "Livelihoods and Communities," Marine Stewardship Council, http://www.msc.org/healthy-oceans/the-oceans-today/livelihoods-communities.

16. "Freshwater Crisis," *National Geographic* online, http://environment.nationalgeographic.com/environment/freshwater/freshwater-crisis/.

17. "Fun Water Facts," Rivers, http://www.rivers.gov/kids/funfacts.html.

18. "Great Lakes: Basic Information," Environmental Protection Agency, http://www.epa.gov/greatlakes/basicinfo.html.

19. "Restoring Rivers: The Lifeblood of Communities," *National Geographic* online, http://environment.nationalgeographic.com/environment/freshwater/rivers/.

20. "Quotes about River," Goodreads.com, http://www.goodreads.com/quotes/tag/river?page=2.

21. "What Is a Salt Marsh?" National Oceanic and Atmospheric Administration, http://oceanservice.noaa.gov/facts/saltmarsh.html.

22. Stephen Foster, Ricardo Hirata, Ana Vidal, Gerhard Schmidt, and Hector Garduño, "The Guarani Aquifer Initiative—Towards Realistic Groundwater Management in a Transboundary Context," Water Partnership Program, Case Profile Collection #9, November 2009, http://www.un-igrac.org/dynamics/modules/SFIL0100/view.php?fil_Id=186.

23. "Fun Water Facts," Rivers, http://www.rivers.gov/kids/funfacts.html.

24. "The Impact of a Cotton T-Shirt: How Smart Choices Can Make a Difference in Our Water and Energy Footprint," World Wildlife (January 13, 2013), http://worldwildlife.org/stories/the-impact-of-a-cotton-t-shirt.

25. Renee Cho, "Wasting Food = Wasting Water," *State of the Planet: The Earth Institute at Columbia University* (blog), (July 1, 2011), http://blogs.ei.columbia.edu/2011/07/01/wasting-food-wasting-water/.

26. "Ocean Acidification: Carbon Dioxide Is Putting Shelled Animals at Risk," *National Geographic* online, http://ocean.nationalgeographic.com/ocean/critical-issues-ocean-acidification/.

27. Kevin Noone, Rashid Sumaila, and Robert J. Diaz, eds., "Valuing the Ocean: Draft Executive Summary," Stockholm Environment Institute, http://www.sei-international.org/mediamanager/documents/Publications/SEI-Preview-ValuingTheOcean-DraftExecutive Summary.pdf.

28. "'Dead Zone' Is a More Common Term for Hypoxia, Which Refers to a Reduced Level of Oxygen in the Water," National Oceanic and Atmospheric Administration (January 23, 2014), http://oceanservice.noaa.gov/facts/deadzone.html.

29. Carolyn Lochhead, "Dead Zone in Gulf Linked to Ethanol Production," *San Francisco Gate* online (July 6, 2010), http://www.sfgate.com/politics/article/Dead-zone-in-gulf-linked-to-ethanol-production-3183032.php.

30. "The Stars Are Aligned for Small Island Developing States," Association of Small Island States (October 13, 2013), http://aosis.org/the-stars-are-aligned-for-small-island-developing-states/.

31. "Oil Pollution," SeaWiFS Project: National Aeronautics and Space Administration (1995), http://seawifs.gsfc.nasa.gov/OCEAN_PLANET/HTML/peril_oil_pollution.html.

32. Ibid.

33. "A Monstrous Mess: Toxic Water Pollution in China," Greenpeace (January 23, 2014), http://www.greenpeace.org/international/en/news/features/A-Monstrous-Mess-toxic-water-pollution-in-China/.

34. Kevin Noone, Rashid Sumaila, and Robert J. Diaz, eds., "Valuing the Ocean: Draft Executive Summary," Stockholm Environment Institute, http://www.sei-international.org/mediamanager/documents/Publications/SEI-Preview-ValuingTheOcean-DraftExecutive Summary.pdf.

35. "Unsustainable Fishing," World Wildlife Fund, http://wwf.panda.org/about_our _earth/blue_planet/problems/problems_fishing/.

36. Daniel D. Richter and Daniel Markewitz, "How Deep Is Soil?" BioScience 45, no. 9 (October 1995): 600–609, http://www.jstor.org/discover/10.2307/1312764?uid=3739808& uid=2&uid=4&uid=3739256&sid=21103761336367.

37. World Economic Forum, "What If the World's Soil Runs Out?" Time online (December 14, 2012), http://world.time.com/2012/12/14/what-if-the-worlds-soil-runs-out/.

38. "The World Factbook," Central Intelligence Agency, https://www.cia.gov/library /publications/the-world-factbook/geos/xx.html.

39. Economic and Social Development Department, "Crop Production and Natural Resource Use," Food and Agriculture Organization of the United Nations, http://www.fao.org /docrep/005/y4252e/y4252e06.htm

40. 24/7 Wall St., "Memo To Congress: 'Buy Land, They Ain't Making Any More of It,'" Time online (January 28, 2009), http://content.time.com/time/business /article/0,8599,1874407,00.html.

41. "Plants," Food and Agriculture Organization of the United Nations, http://www.fao .org/biodiversity/components/plants/en/.

42. "What Is the Smallest Flower in the World?" Library of Congress (August 23, 2010), http://www.loc.gov/rr/scitech/mysteries/smallestflower.html.

43. "List of Largest Plants," Wikipedia, http://en.wikipedia.org/wiki/List_of_largest _plants.

44. John Hollenhorst, "Central Utah's Pando, World's Largest Living Thing, Is Threatened, Scientists Say," Deseret News online (October 7, 2010), http://www.deseretnews.com /article/700071982/Central-Utahs-Pando-worlds-largest-living-thing-is-threatened-scientists -say.html?pg=all, http://www.mnn.com/earth-matters/wilderness-resources/photos/worlds-7 -most-amazing-trees/quaking-aspen-pando.

45. World Economic Forum, "What If the World's Soil Runs Out?" *Time* online (December 14, 2012), http://world.time.com/2012/12/14/what-if-the-worlds-soil-runs-out/.

46. Ibid.

47. Steven Rattner, "The Great Corn Con," *New York Times* online (June 24, 2011), http://www.nytimes.com/2011/06/25/opinion/25Rattner.html?_r=0.

48. *The ICUN Red List of Threatened Species* (website), http://www.iucnredlist.org/.

49. Sarah Graham, "Global Estimates of Endangered Plant Species Triples," *Scientific American* online (November 1, 2002), http://www.scientificamerican.com/article/global -estimate-of-endang/.

50. "Mammals," San Diego Zoo Kids (2014), http://kids.sandiegozoo.org/animals /mammals.

51. "Birds," San Diego Zoo Kids (2014), http://kids.sandiegozoo.org/animals/birds.

52. "Species Numbers (as of Aug 2014)," Reptile Database, http://www.reptile-database .org/db-info/SpeciesStat.html.

53. "Reptiles," San Diego Zoo Kids (2014), http://kids.sandiegozoo.org/animals/reptiles.

54. "Amphibians," San Diego Zoo Kids (2014), http://kids.sandiegozoo.org/animals /amphibians.

55. "AmphibiaWeb Species Numbers," AmphibiaWeb, http://amphibiaweb.org/amphib ian/speciesnums.html.

56. "Insects," San Diego Zoo Kids (2014), http://kids.sandiegozoo.org/animals/insects.

57. "Fun Cheetah Facts for Kids," Science Kids (July 24, 2014), http://www.sciencekids .co.nz/sciencefacts/animals/cheetah.html.

58. "The Humpback Song," Learner, http://www.learner.org/jnorth/tm/hwhale/Singing Humpback.html.

59. "Unforgettable Elephants," Public Broadcasting Service, http://www.pbs.org/wnet /nature/unforgettable/emotions.html.

60. "Facts about Insects and Bugs," Funology (2014), http://www.funology.com/facts -about-insects-and-bugs/.

61. "Celebrating 50 Years of the ICUN Red List," ICUN Red List (January 30, 2014), http://www.iucnredlist.org/news/celebrating-50-years-of-the-iucn-red-list.

62. "Table 1: Numbers of Threatened Species by Major Groups of Organisms (1996–2013)," ICUN Red List (November 21, 2013), http://cmsdocs.s3.amazonaws.com/summarystats/2013_2_RL_Stats_Table1.pdf.

63. "What Are the Major Reasons We Are Losing So Much Biodiversity?" World Wildlife Fund, http://wwf.panda.org/about_our_earth/biodiversity/threatsto_biodiversity/.

64. Peter Raven, "60.2: The Value of Biodiversity," Biodiversity (New York: MacGraw-Hill, 2010), https://www.inkling.com/read/biology-peter-raven-9th/chapter-60/the-value-of-biodiversity.

65. "The Importance of Biodiversity," Quebec Biodiversity Website, http://redpath-museum.mcgill.ca/Qbp/2.About%20Biodiversity/importance.html#non-humans.

66. Ibid.

67. "Commute Statistics," Statistic Brain.com (January 1, 2014), http://www.statistic brain.com/commute-statistics/.

68. "The Atmosphere," National Aeronautics and Space Administration (June 12, 2014), https://www.grc.nasa.gov/www/k-12/airplane/atmosphere.html.

69. "Argon," Merriam-Webster Online, http://www.merriam-webster.com/dictionary /argon.

70. Fred Rosner, "Moses Maimonides' Treatise on Asthma," Thorax 36 (1981): 245–51, http://thorax.bmj.com/content/36/4/245.full.pdf.

71. Joseph Stromberg, "Air Pollution Has Been a Problem Since the Days of Ancient Rome," Smithsonian Magazine online (February 2013), http://www.smithsonianmag.com /history/air-pollution-has-been-a-problem-since-the-days-of-ancient-rome-3950678/?no-ist.

72. "The Great Smog of 1952," Met Office, http://www.metoffice.gov.uk/education /teens/case-studies/great-smog.

73. Don Hopey, "Museum Remembers Donora's Deadly 1948 Smog," Pittsburgh Post -Gazette online (October 21, 2008), http://www.post-gazette.com/neighborhoods/2008/10/21 /Museum-remembers-Donora-s-deadly-1948-smog/stories/200810210140.

74. Jennifer Chu, "Air Pollution Causes 200,000 Early Deaths Each Year in the U.S.," Laboratory for Aviation and the Environment, Massachusetts Institute of Technology (August 29, 2013), http://web.mit.edu/newsoffice/2013/study-air-pollution-causes-200000-early-deaths-each -year-in-the-us-0829.html.

75. Aaron Cantú, "Disturbing New Report: Air Pollution Killed 7 Million People in 2012—or about 1 in 8 Premature Deaths." AlterNet (March 26, 2014), http://www.alternet

.org/environment/disturbing-new-report-air-pollution-killed-7-million-people-2012-or-about-1-8-premature.

76. "Six Common Air Pollutants," Environmental Protection Agency (April 20, 2012), http://www.epa.gov/air/urbanair/.

77. Greg Toppo, "Childhood Lead Exposure Linked to Adult Crime," *USA Today* online (May 28, 2008), http://usatoday30.usatoday.com/news/health/2008-05-27-lead-levels-crime_N.htm?csp=1.

78. Linda Gorman, "The Impact of Childhood Lead Exposure on Adult Crime," National Bureau of Economic Research, http://www.nber.org/digest/may08/w13097.html.

79. "International Programme on Chemical Safety: Lead," World Health Organization, http://www.who.int/ipcs/assessment/public_health/lead/en/.

80. "The Clean Air Act and the Economy," Environmental Protection Agency, http://www.epa.gov/cleanairactbenefits/economy.html#backtowork.

81. Ibid., http://www.epa.gov/cleanairactbenefits/economy.html#CAAspares.

82. Robert Kunzig, "Climate Milestone: Earth's CO_2 Level Passes 400 ppm," *National Geographic* online (May 9, 2013), http://news.nationalgeographic.com/news/energy/2013/05/130510-earth-co2-milestone-400-ppm/.

83. James Hansen, "Target Atmosphere CO_2: Where Should Humanity Aim?" Cornell University Library (October 15, 2008), http://arxiv.org/abs/0804.1126.

84. Richard Matthews, "What Is Environmental Migration and Who Are Climate Refugees?" Green Conduct, http://greenconduct.com/news/2013/06/02/what-is-environmental-migration-and-who-are-climate-refugees/.

85. R. L. Miller, "Climate Change Report Supports Bill McKibben's 'Terrifying New Math,'" Take Part (September 28, 2013), http://www.takepart.com/article/2013/09/27/ipcc-report-climate-change-bill-mckibben-new-math.

86. Ibid.

87. Christian Aid, "Taken by Storm: Responding to the Impacts of Climate Change," Christian Aid (March 2014), http://www.christianaid.org.uk/Images/Taken-by-storm-climate-change-report-march-2014.pdf.

88. Suzanne Goldenberg, "Meet America's First Climate Refugees," *Mother Jones* online (May 30, 2013), http://www.motherjones.com/environment/2013/05/americas-first-climate-refugees-newtok-alaska.

89. John Vidal, "Global Warming Could Create 150 Million 'Climate Refugees' by 2050," *Guardian* online (November 2, 2009), http://www.theguardian.com/environment/2009 /nov/03/global-warming-climate-refugees.

90. "Stabilization Wedges," Princeton University, http://cmi.princeton.edu/wedges/.

7. A New Green Revolution

1. For more information, see "Alliance of Religions and Conservation—History," Alliance of Religions and Conservation, http://www.arcworld.org/about.asp?pageID=2#86.

2. See examples at "Welcome to Our Muslim GreenWorship Resource!" GreenFaith, http://greenfaith.org/resource-center/spirit/greenworship-resource/muslim-greenworship -resource.

3. Qur'an 4:43, Ali Quli Qara'i, *The Qur'an: With a Phrase-by-Phrase English Translation* (London: ICAS Press, 2004), http://al-quran.info/#4:43.

4. "Welcome to Our Muslim GreenWorship Resource!" GreenFaith, http://greenfaith .org/resource-center/spirit/greenworship-resource/muslim-greenworship-resource/welcome -to-our-muslim-greenworship-resource#tip-2-practice-tayammum.

5. Meredith Sabini, "The Earth Has a Soul," Ecological Buddhism, http://www.ecobud dhism.org/wisdom/psyche_and_spirit/sabini_jung/.

6. "Fast Facts about American Religion," Hartford Institute for Religion Research, http:// hirr.hartsem.edu/research/fastfacts/fast_facts.html.

7. "Frequently Requested Church Statistics," Center for Applied Research in the Apostolate: Georgetown University, http://cara.georgetown.edu/caraservices/requestedchurchstats .html.

8. Caroline Pomeroy, review of *Ecological Identity: Becoming a Reflective Environmentalist* by Mitchell Thomashow (Massachusetts Institute of Technology Press, 1995), http://jpe .library.arizona.edu/volume_2/pomeroyvol2.htm.

9. Secretary-General Ban ki Moon, "Speech to Summit of Religious Leaders on Climate Change," November 3, 2009, Windsor Castle, England.

10. Ibid.

11. "Success Story: Temple Beth Rishon," Energy Star, http://www.energystar.gov/ia /business/small_business/sb_success/sb_successstories_temple_beth_rishon.html.

12. "Putting Energy Into Stewardship," Energy Star, http://www.energystar.gov/sites /default/files/buildings/tools/2013_Congregations_Poster.pdf.

13. Annysa Johnson, "Milwaukee Event to Showcase Religion's Role in Water Conservation," *Journal Sentinel* online (January 24, 2014), http://www.jsonline.com/news/religion /milwaukee-event-to-showcase-religions-role-in-water-conservation-b99190462z1 -241878221.html.

14. "Adamah," Hazon, http://hazon.org/adamah/.

15. Abstract of "Body and Soul. A Dietary Intervention Conducted through African-American Churches," National Center for Biotechnology Information, http://www.ncbi.nlm .nih.gov/pubmed/15261895.

16. Gadadhara Padit Dasa, http://www.nycpandit.com/activities.html

17. Thornton McEnery, "The World's 15 Biggest Landowners," Business Insider (March 18, 2011), http://www.businessinsider.com/worlds-biggest-landowners-2011-3?op=1.

18. "Putting Energy Into Stewardship," Energy Star, http://www.energystar.gov/sites /default/files/buildings/tools/2013_Congregations_Poster.pdf.

19. Allen Johnson, "The Endangered Species Act: A Modern Noah's Ark," *Christian Post* online (April 3, 2014), http://www.christianpost.com/news/the-endangered-species-act-a -modern-noahs-ark-117299/.

20. Mitchell C. Hescox, "Caring for God's Creation Is Pro-Life," Evangelical Environmental Network (April 14, 2014), http://www.creationcare.org/category.php?blog=1&category =20.

21. "EPA Fact Sheet: Reducing Carbon Emissions from Power Plants: Moving Forward on the Climate Action Plan," Environmental Protection Agency (September 20, 2013), http:// www2.epa.gov/sites/production/files/2013-09/documents/20130920factsheet.pdf.

22. Zachary Cikanek, "API Welcomes High Court Decision to Review EPA Carbon Rules," American Petroleum Institute (October 15, 2013), http://www.api.org/news-and -media/news/newsitems/2013/oct-2013/api-welcomes-high-court-decision-to-review-epa -carbon-rules.

23. Frederick Butler, "Interfaith Power & Light Lauds New EPA Safeguards for Power Plants as Protecting Cration," Interfaith Power & Light (September 20, 2013), http://www .interfaithpowerandlight.org/2013/09/interfaith-power-light-lauds-new-epa-safeguards-for -power-plants-as-protecting-creation/.

24. "Facilities," Covanta, http://www.covanta.com/facilities/facility-by-location/essex .aspx.

25. Office of Science, "Mercury Emissions," State of New Jersey Department of Environmental Protection (March 2013), http://www.nj.gov/dep/dsr/trends/pdfs/mercury.pdf.

26. Eliot Caroom, "Newark Incinerator Plant to Get Cleaner Emissions Controls," *Star-Ledger* online (September 16, 2012), http://www.nj.com/business/index.ssf/2012/09/newark_incinerator_plant_to_ge.html.

27. Ironbound Community Corp., and GreenFaith, Inc. v. Covanta Essex Co., Covanta Energy Corporation, and Covanta Holding Corporation, declaration of Sister Eleanor Uhl, O.P., in US District Court for the District of New Jersey, Feb. 18, 2009.

28. "Ironbound Community Corporation and GreenFaith Announce Settlement," GreenFaith (October 1, 2010), http://greenfaith.org/media/press-releases/ironbound-community-corporation-and-greenfaith-announce-settlement.

29. Eliot Caroom, "Newark Incinerator Plant to Get Cleaner Emissions Controls," *Star-Ledger* online (September 16, 2012), http://www.nj.com/business/index.ssf/2012/09/newark_incinerator_plant_to_ge.html.

30. Katherine Bagley, "The Most Influential Climate Science Paper Today Remains Unknown to Most People," Inside Climate News (February 14, 2013), https://insideclimatenews.org/news/20140213/climate-change-science-carbon-budget-nature-global-warming-2-degrees-bill-mckibben-fossil-fuels-keystone-xl-oil?page=show.

31. Fiona Harvey, "IPCC: 30 years to climate calamity if we carry on blowing the carbon budget," *The Guardian* online (September 27, 2013), http://www.theguardian.com/environment/2013/sep/27/ipcc-world-dangerous-climate-change.

32. "Carbon Bubble," Carbon Tracker, http://www.carbontracker.org/carbonbubble.

33. Jessica Leber, "Are Oil Companies Wasting Billions on Energy They'll Never Use?" Fast Co.Exist (October 28, 2023), http://www.fastcoexist.com/3020656/are-oil-companies-wasting-billions-on-energy-theyll-never-use.

34. "Global Treands in Renewable Energy Investment 2013," Frankfort School FS-UNEP Collaborating Centre for Climate & Sustainable Energy Finance, http://fs-unep-centre.org/publications/global-trends-renewable-energy-investment-2013.

35. "Energy Subsidies," International Energy Agency, http://www.iea.org/publications/worldenergyoutlook/resources/energysubsidies/.

36. "Oil & Gas," Open Secrets (July 24, 2014), http://www.opensecrets.org/industries/indus.php?Ind=E01.

37. Bill McKibben, "Global Warming's Terrifying New Math," *Rolling Stone* online (July 19, 2012), http://www.rollingstone.com/politics/news/global-warmings-terrifying-new -math-20120719.

38. Ibid.

39. Petition "Divest New Haven from Fossil Fuels," Fossil Free, http://campaigns.go fossilfree.org/petitions/divest-new-haven-from-fossil-fuels.

40. Doug Demeo, "Getting Out of Oil," *America Magazine* online (April 21, 2014), http://americamagazine.org/issue/getting-out-oil.

41. Damian Carrington, "Desmond Tutu Calls for Anti-Apartied Style Boycott of Fossil Fuel Industry," *Guardian* online (April 10, 2014), http://www.theguardian.com/environ ment/2014/apr/10/desmond-tutu-anti-apartheid-style-boycott-fossil-fuel-industry.

42. Atif Ansar, Ben Caldecott, and James Tilsbury, "Stranded Assets and the Fossil Fuel Divestment Campaign: What Does Divestment Mean for the Valuation of Fossil Fuel Assets?" Smith School of Enterprise and the Environment: University of Oxford, http://www.smith school.ox.ac.uk/research/stranded-assets/SAP-divestment-report-final.pdf.

43. "GreenFaith Certification Program," GreenFaith., http://greenfaith.org/programs /certification.

8. Our Kairos Moment

1. E. C. White, *Kaironomia: On the Will to Invent* (Ithaca and London: Cornell University Press, 1987), 13.

2. Jonathan Kaiman, "China's Reliance on Coal Reduces Life Expectancy by 5.5 Years, Says Study," *Guardian* online (July 8, 2013), http://www.theguardian.com/environment/2013 /jul/08/northern-china-air-pollution-life-expectancy.

3. "7 Million Premature Deaths Annually Linked to Air Pollution," World Health Organization (March 25, 2014), http://www.who.int/mediacentre/news/releases/2014/air-pollu tion/en/.

4. Margaret Chan, "WHO Director-General Addresses Budapest Water Summit," World Health Organization (October 9, 2013), http://www.who.int/dg/speeches/2013/water_sanita tion/en/.

5. "Warmer World Will Keep Millions of People Trapped in Poverty, Says New Report," World Bank (June 19, 2013), http://www.worldbank.org/en/news/press-release/2013/06/19 /warmer-world-will-keep-millions-of-people-trapped-in-poverty-says-new-report.

6. Ibid.

7. United Nations Environment Programme, "Green Jobs: Toward Decent Work in a Sustainable, Low-Carbon World," International Labour Organization (September 2008), http://www.ilo.org/wcmsp5/groups/public/@ed_emp/@emp_ent/documents/publication /wcms_158733.pdf.

8. Robert Pollin, "Doing the Recovery Right," *Nation* (February 16, 2009).

9. Jorge Madrid and Adam James, "Bureau of Labor Statistics Reports 3.1 Million U.S. Green Jobs: Top 5 Takeaways," Think Progress (March 23, 2012), http://thinkprogress.org /climate/2012/03/23/450776/bureau-of-labor-statistics-reports-31-million-us-green-jobs -top-5-takeaways/.

10. Robert Pollin, "Doing the Recovery Right," *Nation* (February 16, 2009).

11. Madrid and James, http://thinkprogress.org/climate/2012/03/23/450776/bureau-of -labor-statistics-reports-31-million-us-green-jobs-top-5-takeaways/.

12. Jennifer Runyon, "US Solar Jobs Growing Ten Times Faster Than National Average Employment Growth," Renewable Energy World (January 27, 2014), http://www.renew ableenergyworld.com/rea/news/article/2014/01/solar-jobs-growing-ten-times-faster-than -national-average-employment-growth.

13. Ibid.

14. "Fast Facts," Vote Solar, http://votesolar.org/fact-room/fast-facts/.

15. Bobby Magill, "New Map Shows Explosive Growth of U.S. Wind Energy," Weather Underground (March 27, 2014), http://www.wunderground.com/news/new-map-shows -explosive-growth-wind-energy-across-us-20140327.

16. Robert Pollin, "Doing the Recovery Right," *Nation* (February 16, 2009).

17. Gene Balas, "A More Direct Approach to Unemployment," *Real Money* (February 6, 2012), http://realmoney.thestreet.com/articles/02/06/2012/more-direct-approach-unemploy ment.

18. Thich Nhat Hanh, *Touching Peace: Practicing the Art of Mindful Living* (Berkeley, CA: Parallex Press, 1992); also at http://www.goodreads.com/work/quotes/850642-touching -peace-practicing-the-art-of-mindful-living.

19. Eliza Barclay, "Prison Gardens Help Inmates Grow Their Own Food—and Skills," National Public Radio (January 12, 2014), http://www.npr.org/blogs/the salt/2014/01/12/261397333/prison-gardens-help-inmates-grow-their-own-food-and-skills.

20. Ken Tanner, "Does Natural Lighting Influence Student Achievement?" University of Georgia (April 2000), http://sdpl.coe.uga.edu/researchabstracts/naturallight.html.

21. C. Kenneth Tanner, "Explaining Relationships Among Student Outcomes and the School's Physical Environment," *Journal of Advanced Academics* 2008, vol. 19, no. 3 (May 2008), doi: 10.4219/jaa-2008-812, http://joa.sagepub.com/content/19/3/444.full .pdf+html?ijkey=O.MGWgkP51ptY&keytype=ref&siteid=spjoa

22. Lawrence St. Leger, "Health and Nature—New Challenges for Health Promotion," *Health Promotion International* 18, no. 3 (2003): 173–75, http://heapro.oxfordjournals.org /content/18/3/173.full.

23. Ibid.

24. "Climate Refugee," National Geographic online, http://education.nationalgeographic .com/education/encyclopedia/climate-refugee/?ar_a=1.

CPSIA information can be obtained
at www.ICGtesting.com
Printed in the USA
FSHW021323030419
56925FS